Guido Norman Lieber

Remarks on the Army Regulations and Executive Regulations in General

Guido Norman Lieber

Remarks on the Army Regulations and Executive Regulations in General

ISBN/EAN: 9783337111823

Printed in Europe, USA, Canada, Australia, Japan

Cover: Foto ©Andreas Hilbeck / pixelio.de

More available books at **www.hansebooks.com**

REMARKS

ON

THE ARMY REGULATIONS

AND

EXECUTIVE REGULATIONS IN GENERAL.

BY

G. NORMAN LIEBER,
JUDGE-ADVOCATE GENERAL,
U. S. ARMY.

WASHINGTON:
GOVERNMENT PRINTING OFFICE.
1898.

WAR DEPARTMENT.
Document No. 63.
OFFICE OF THE JUDGE-ADVOCATE GENERAL.

TABLE OF CONTENTS.

CHAPTER I.

Classification and Source of Authority of Army Regulations 5

CHAPTER II.

Executive Regulations in General 21

CHAPTER III.

Approval of Regulations by Congress 51

CHAPTER IV.

The Different Editions of Army Regulations 61

CHAPTER V.

The Interpretation and Construction of Regulations 85

Appendix A.—Letter of the Secretary of War with regard to General Order No. 32, Adjutant-General's Office, 1873 103

Appendix B.—Extract from the Judge-Advocate General's remarks on revocable licenses 121

Appendix C.—Opinion of Hon. J. M. Dickinson with reference to the constitutionality of the act of Congress giving the Secretary of War powers in regard to obstructions to navigation 129

Appendix D.—Extract from the Regulations for the Revenue-Cutter Service 139

	Page.
APPENDIX E.—Explanation of General Scott with reference to the Army Regulations of 1821	145
APPENDIX F.—Letter of Secretary of War Belknap, accompanying proposed regulations of 1873	149
APPENDIX G.—Report of Military Committee of the House of Representatives, Forty-third Congress, first session, on "Revised Army Regulations"	151
APPENDIX H.—Letter of General Schofield in regard to proposed regulations of 1876	185
APPENDIX I. Remarks of Secretary of War McCrary in his annual report of 1877	187

CHAPTER I.

CLASSIFICATION AND SOURCE OF AUTHORITY OF ARMY REGULATIONS.

The words *regulate* and *regulation* are used in several places in the Constitution of the United States. Thus, Congress has power to "regulate" commerce, to "regulate" the value of money, to make rules for the government and "regulation" of the land and naval forces, to make "regulations" with regard to the elections of Senators and Representatives, to make "regulations" with reference to the jurisdiction of the Supreme Court in certain cases, and to make needful rules and "regulations" respecting the territory and other property of the United States. In all these cases regulation is legislation.

By virtue of its power to make rules and regulations for the land and naval forces, Congress covers a large field of legislation relating to the administration of military affairs. When this is done, there, however, remains a mass of matters appertaining to the military establishment, which it is necessary to "regulate." Legislation can not enter into all the details of this regulation, and, if it could, it would not be desirable, because a legislative code, controlling the whole subject of military administration, would not have the necessary elasticity. The Constitution provides a way of supplementing this power of Congress, the President, as Executive and Commander-in-Chief of the Army, having the power to make regulations for its government.¹

The regulations for the transaction of the public duties and business relating to the military establishment, adopted by the President in the exercise of this power, are designated as the Army Regulations. They may be divided into several classes, viz:

1. Those which have received the sanction of Congress. These cannot be altered, nor can exceptions to them be made, by the executive authority, unless the regulations themselves provide for it. In reality, the approval of Congress makes them legislative regulations, and they might therefore be more strictly classified with other statutory regulations with reference to subjects of military administration. They are, however, included under the general head of Army Regulations, as approved codes of executive regulations. Examples of regulations having this sanction are given *post*.

2. Those that are made pursuant to, or in execution of, a statute—meaning by the latter expression, those that are supplemental to particular statutes, and, in

---

¹ "*Regulations* are administrative rules or directions as distinguished from enactments. They exist in all the Executive Departments and are of very material service in the efficient administration of the Government. *Army regulations* are authoritative directions as to the details of military duty and discipline. The authority for Army regulations is to be found in the distinctive functions of the President as Commander in Chief and as Executive. His function as Commander in Chief authorizes him to issue, personally or through his military subordinates, such orders and directions as are necessary and proper to insure order and discipline in the Army. His function as Executive empowers him, personally or through the Secretary of War, to prescribe rules, where requisite, for the due execution of the statutes relating to the military establishment." (Winthrop's Abridgment of Military Law, p. 8.)

the absence of sufficient legislative regulation, prescribe means for carrying them out. These, if it be not prohibited by the statute, may be modified by the executive authority,[1] but until this is done they are binding as well on the authority that made them as on others. It has been held that a regulation of the Treasury Department, made in pursuance of an act of Congress, "becomes a part of the law, and of as binding force as if incorporated in the body of the act itself."[2] So it has been held that the civil service rules, promulgated under the Civil Service Act, "became a part of the law," and that removal from a position placed under the act and the rules can only be made agreeably to the terms and provisions of both the act and the rules,[3] and an Army regulation made pursuant

---

[1] "The power to establish implies, necessarily, the power to modify or repeal, or to create anew." (United States v. Eliason, 16 Pet., 302.)

[2] United States v. Barrows, 1 Abbott, 351; 24 Fed. Cases, 1018.

[3] Butler v. White, 83 Fed. Rep., 578. See also United States v. Wade, 75 Fed. Rep., 264; Boody v. United States, 3 Fed. Cases, 860; United States v. Webster, 28 Fed. Cases, 509; Allen v. Colby, 47 N. H., 544; The Thomas Gibbons, 8 Cr., 421; Parker v. United States, 1 P., 293, 297; United States v. Freeman, 25 Fed. Cases, 1211; Lockington's Case, Bright. 269; Low v. Hanson, 72 Me., 104; United States v. Williams, 6 Mont., 379; Caha v. United States, 152 U. S., 211, 221. But as to the conclusion in Butler v. White, in regard to removals from office under the civil service act and rules, see *post*, p. 29, note.

By act of Congress of March 1, 1823, it was prescribed, "That if any persons shall swear or affirm falsely, touching the expenditure of public money, or in support of any claim against the United States, he or she shall, upon conviction thereof, suffer as for willful and corrupt perjury." It was held by the Supreme Court that under this legislation the Secretary of the Treasury had the power to make a regulation authorizing justices of the peace of States to administer oaths to affidavits in support of claims, and that perjury might be assigned on an affidavit so taken, (United States v. Bailey, 9 Pet., 238). And see United States v. Breen, 40 Fed. Rep., 402.

to a provision contained in an act of Congress is of the
same force. Examples of regulations of this class are
those relating to the examination of enlisted men for
commissions, under the act of Congress of July 30,
1892, and the Executive order of March 30, 1898, prescribing limits of punishment.

3. Those emanating from, and depending on, the

<small>Such regulations must of course be consistent with the law, as is pointed out in the following extract from a report of the Judge-Advocate General's Office, dated November 22, 1888.

"Paragraph 2454, Army Regulations of 1881, was first promulgated by direction of the Secretary of War on June 22, 1872, in General Orders No. 51, A. G. O. These orders prescribed rules for the execution of the provisions of the act of Congress approved May 15, 1872 (17 Stat., 116), now embraced in sections 1280–1284, Revised Statutes. Although this statute was silent as to the execution of the details of its provisions, yet as the execution thereof, from the nature of the enactment, required to be specifically methodized, the authority for prescribing rules to effectuate the objects of the law resulted by legal implication in connection with the constitutional duty of the executive department to 'take care that the laws be faithfully executed.' (1 Winthrop, 19; McCall's Case, 2 Phila., 269; 10 Wheat., 42; 7 Pet., 2; 9 *id.*, 238; 1 Pet., C. C., 471; 1 W. & M., 164; 11 Mich., 298; 16 Wis., 423; 5 Phila., 287; 47 N. H., 544; Cooley's Principles Constitutional Law, 44; 1 Opin. Atty. Gen., 478; 2 *id.*, 225, 243–245, 421; 4 *id.*, 225, 227; 6 *id.*, 365; 16 *id.*, 39.)

"It is obvious that the regulations under discussion were made in aid of the law cited and therefore belong to the class of regulations termed by the Court of Claims in its opinion, heretofore mentioned, as ' supplementary to the statutes which have been enacted by Congress in reference to the Army.' But in order that such regulations shall have the force of law, they must, under the authorities cited, be *consistent* with the statute in aid of which they were made.

"It will appear from the report of this office of October 9, 1888, that paragraph 2454, Army Regulations of 1881, was originally issued under a misapprehension of the intent and effect of the provisions of the act of Congress approved May 15, 1872 (see. 1280–1284, Rev. Stat.). To make this paragraph *consistent* with the statute a project for an amendment was submitted and substantially adopted by the Secretary of War by the publication of General Orders No. 95, of November 10, 1888, amending Army Regulation, 2454."

See also Dig. Opin. Judge-Advocate General, 168.</small>

constitutional authority of the President as Commander-in-Chief of the Army and as Executive, and not made in supplement to particular statutes. These constitute the greater part of the Army regulations. They are not only modified at will by the President, but exemptions from particular regulations are given in exceptional cases; the exercise of this power with reference to them being found necessary. "The authority which makes them (regulations) can modify or suspend them as to any case, or class of cases, or generally."[1]

---

[1] 5 Dec. First Comptroller, 29, and see art. 1 of Circ. No. 4, 1897, A. G. O.; Circ. No. 2, 1885; United States v. Eliason, 16 Pet., 302; Davis's Military Laws, 146, and Military Law, 6; 3 Dec. Comp. Treas., 305; Smith v. United States, 24 Ct. Cls., 209; Arthur v. United States, 16 Ct. Cls., 422; Opin. Judge-Advocate General, March 5, 1896, concurred in by the War Department (2074).

The following is an extract from the opinion last cited:

"Regulations may be divided into different classes with respect to this question. There are, or may be, those which have received the sanction of Congress, and it is evident that the Secretary of War would have no authority to make an exception to one of these. There are also those that are made pursuant to and in aid of a statute. These may be modified, but, until this is done, are binding as well on the authority that made them as on others. (United States v. Barrows, 1 Abbott, 351). There is also a large body of other regulations emanating from, and depending solely on the authority of the President as Commander in Chief. With reference to such regulations, it has, I believe, been sometimes claimed that the same rule should be applied that is applied to the regulations made pursuant to statute. But this has not been done in practice, and I do not think that it should be done, for the reason that it would seem to be an unnecessary, embarrassing, and perhaps unconstitutional limitation of the authority of the President as Commander in Chief. To exempt from compliance with a particular regulation in an exceptional case would seem to be a lawful exercise of that authority."

In United States v. Burns, 12 Wall., 246, the Supreme Court held with reference to an Army regulation, prohibiting persons in the military service from making contracts for supplies, etc., with other persons in the military service, that the regulation did not apply to contracts on behalf of the United States, which required for their validity the approval of the Secretary of War;

To which are sometimes added:

4. Departmental regulations, made by virtue of the authority conferred by section 161, Revised Statutes, on the head of each Department "to prescribe regulations not inconsistent with law, for the government of his Department, the conduct of its officers and clerks, the distribution and performance of its business, and the custody, use, and preservation of its records, papers, and property appertaining thereto."[1]

Mere repetitions of legislative enactments are not included under any of these heads.

A long continued practice has been held equivalent to a specific regulation.[2]

---

that though contracts of that character are usually negotiated by subordinate officers or agents of the Government, they are in fact and in law the acts of the Secretary, whose sanction is essential to bind the United States; and that the Secretary, though the head of the War Department, is not in the military service in the sense of the regulation, but, on the contrary, is a civil officer with civil duties to perform, as much as the head of any other of the Executive Departments. This decision is sometimes referred to as sustaining the view that Army regulations are not in any case binding on the authority that makes them, whereas all that was held is that the regulation in question was not intended to restrain the Secretary of War. (See the case of Smith v. United States, 24 Ct. Cls., 209.)

[1] Section 1059, Revised Statutes, vests the Court of Claims with jurisdiction to hear and determine claims founded upon any regulation of an Executive Department, which the court has construed as meaning any regulation within the lawful discretion of the head of an Executive Department. (20 Ct. Cls., 199.)

See also act of March 3, 1887, "to provide for the bringing of suits against the Government of the United States."

[2] United States v. Macdaniel, 7 Pet., 1; United States v. Webster, 28 Fed. Cases, 515; 3 Dec. Comp. Treas., 316.

See also Martin v. Mott, 12 W. 19, and United States v. Babcock, 24 Fed. Cases, 928.

"A regulation is a rule. It may be written, and no reason is perceived why it may not exist in parol or by usage." (Decision First Comptroller, Vol. V, p. 311.) The "custom of war," that is to say, the custom of the service, is recognized by the eighty-fourth Article of War as being a part of the law military.

As to the subject-matter of regulations for the government of the Army, no distinct line can be drawn

But usage can not be relied on in justification of an act forbidden by express law. (Walker v. The Transportation Company, 3 Wall., 150; Clark's Browne on Usages and Customs, p. 27, note; 27 Am. and Eng. Enc. of Law, 798.) A noticeable instance of the disregard of this principle is to be found in a work on "The Military Law of England," published in London in 1810, in which, after stating the law relating to duelling, as contained in the Articles of War, it is said that "there are cases in which, notwithstanding the explicit declarations of the written law, the custom of the service would seem to demand a reference to arms," and, accordingly, "General Rules and Instructions for Seconds in Duels" are given.

"A usage or custom, at military law, must consist of a fixed and uniform practice of long standing, which is not in conflict with existing statute law or regulation. A custom of the service can not be established by proof of isolated or occasional instances, but must be built up out of a series of precedents. It must also be a usage of the Army, or of some separate and distinct branch of the military establishment. Moreover, no illegal or unauthorized practice, however frequent or long continued, can make a usage." (Winthrop's Abridgment of Military Law, p. 14.)

In connection with the above classification of Army regulations, see the decision of the Court of Claims in Maj. William Smith's Case, 23 Ct. Cls., 452, in which the court said:

"The Constitution provides, in Article I, section 8, paragraph 14, that Congress shall have power 'to make rules for the government and regulation of the land and naval forces.'

"It has been argued here and elsewhere that this provision deprives the President of authority to make such rules of his own motion, or even when previously authorized by legislative action, on the ground that the power is exclusive in Congress and can not be delegated; and so that all rules for the government and regulation of the land and naval forces made by the Executive are void and of no effect without the enactment by Congress in the form of approval or otherwise.

"Congress has established rules and articles for the government of the armies of the United States, commonly called 'Articles of War' (act of April 10, 1806, chapter 20, 2 Stat. L., 359, now Rev. Stat., sec. 1342).

"For the making of other and ordinary regulations Congress has from an early day proceeded upon the idea that the power might be delegated to the President, and has passed several acts expressly conferring such authority (act of March 3, 1813, chapter 52, section 5 (2 Stat. L., 819); act of April 24, 1816, chapter 69, section 9 (3 Stat. L., 298); act July 15, 1870, chapter 294, section 20 (16 Stat. L., 319); act of March 1, 1875, chapter 115 (Supp.

separating the President's constitutional power to make them from the constitutional power of Congress

Rev. Stat., 149), and the act of June 23, 1879, chapter 35, section 2 (Supp. Rev. Stat., 494), under which the edition of 1881 was published.)

"Congress has three times recognized or approved existing regulations:

"1. The act of April 24, 1816, chapter 69, section 9 (3 Stat. L., 298), provided that 'the regulations in force before the reduction of the Army be recognized, as far as the same shall be found applicable to the service, subject, however, to such alterations as the Secretary of War may adopt, with the approbation of the President.'

"2. The act of March 2, 1821, chapter 13, section 14 (3 Stat. L., 616), enacted 'that the system of "general regulations for the Army" compiled by Major General Scott shall be, and the same is hereby, approved and adopted for the government of the Army of the United States and of the militia, when in the service of the United States.' This section was unconditionally repealed by the act of May 7, 1822, chapter 88 (3 Stat. L., 686). As to this act Attorney General Wirt advised that, notwithstanding such repeal, the regulations having received the sanction of the President, continued in force by the authority of the President in all cases where they did not conflict with positive legislation. (1 Opin., 549).

"3. The act of July 28, 1866, chapter 299, section 37 (14 Stat. L., 337, 338), required the Secretary of War to prepare a code of regulations for the government of the Army, and enacted 'the existing regulations to remain in force until Congress shall have acted on said report.' No such action has been taken.

"It is well settled that Army regulations when directly approved by Congress have the absolute force of law equally with other legislative acts until repealed by the same power. Congress so treated them when it passed the act of June 8, 1872, chapter 348 (17 Stat. L., 337), providing that the fifth section of the act of May 8, 1872 (17 Stat. L., 83), should not be held to repeal that part of paragraph 1030 of the Revised Army Regulations of 1863 with which it appeared to be in conflict, thus recognizing the regulations approved by Congress in that year as having the same force as Congressional enactments.

"On the other hand, it is just as well settled that regulations not so approved have the force of law only when founded on the President's constitutional powers as Commander in Chief of the Army, or are 'consistent with and supplementary to the statutes which have been enacted by Congress in reference to the Army.' (Symond's Case, 120 U. S., 46, affirming 21 Ct. Cls., 151; Reed's Case, 100 U. S., 22; Smith v. Whitney, 116 id., 180; United States v. Whitney, 120 id., 47; Wayman v. Southard, 10 Wheat., 43;

"to make rules for the government and regulation" of the land forces. Regulations are, when they relate

United States *v.* Eliason, 16 Pet., 291; United States *v.* Freeman, 3 How., 556; Kurtz *v.* Moffitt, 115 U. S., 503; United States *v.* Webster, 2 Ware, 66; United States *v.* Maurice, 2 Brock, 103; Ferren's Case, 3 Benedict, 447; Gates *v.* Fletcher, 1 Minn., 204; 1 Opin. Atty. Gen., 469, 547; 2 *id.*, 225; 3 *id.*, 85; 6 *id.*, 10, 215, 365; 10 *id.*, 415; 16 *id.*, 38.)

"Whether a regulation, the validity of which is drawn in question, is within the constitutional power of the President to promulgate, or whether it has been approved by Congress, or whether it 'is consistent with and supplementary to the statutes,' are judicial questions not always free from difficulties of determination.

"In the light of these views and the adjudicated cases we shall examine the existing regulations.

"The present regulations are contained in the edition of 1881, published under authority of the act of March 1, 1875, chapter 115 (Supp. Rev. Stat., 149), which directs the President 'to make and publish regulations for the government of the Army in accordance with existing laws,' and under the act of June 23, 1879, chapter 35, section 2 (Supp. Rev. Stat., 494), which further directs the President to 'cause all the regulations of the Army and general orders now in force to be codified and published to the Army,' and provides for the expenses of the work.

"As promulgated in this edition they contain orders and regulations of four different classes intermingled. At the end of each the earlier authority for it is specified by a note in brackets.

"1. General orders which he (the President) has a right to issue under his constitutional prerogative of 'Commander in Chief of the Army and Navy of the United States.' (Constitution, Art. II, sec. 2, par. 1.)

"2. Departmental regulations, under section 161, Revised Statutes, authorizing the head of each Department to 'prescribe regulations, not inconsistent with law, for the government of his Department, the conduct of officers and clerks, the distribution and performance of its business, and the custody, use, and preservation of its records, papers, and property appertaining thereto.'

"3. Regulations not approved by Congress, but made by the President in the exercise of legislative authority conferred by the acts above cited.

"4. Regulations expressly approved by Congress."

The executive regulations of the British military administration consist, principally, of the Rules of Procedure, the Queen's Regulations, Royal Warrants, and Orders in Council. The Rules of Procedure are authorized by the Army Act, and prescribe the regulations for the formation of military courts, the trial of

to subjects within the constitutional jurisdiction of Congress, unquestionably of a legislative character,

offenders, and the execution of sentences; the Queen's Regulations relate to the interior economy of corps, the maintenance of discipline, and the powers and duties of commanding officers, and supplement the Army Act as to offences against enlistment and the disposal of prisoners; Royal Warrants prescribe the permanent regulations as to the government, discipline, pay, promotion, and conditions of service; and Orders in Council are regulations made by the Crown with the advice of the Privy Council, in regard to matters of great importance, such as the duties of the military when on board public ships, the duties of the office of commander-in-chief and other great military offices, etc. Royal Warrants, General Orders (affecting duty, discipline, and general efficiency), and amendments of the Queen's Regulations, are published in Army Orders. Besides the above there are separate regulations for the Militia, Yeomanry, and Volunteer Forces. (Pratt's Military Law, London, 1892; Gunter's Outlines of Military Law, 1897.)

Until toward the close of the last century there appears to have been no authorized system of general army regulations in existence in England, each colonel having his own standing orders for the discipline and exercise of the regiment, so that "there was not any standard of uniformity or of efficiency by which progress in the military art could be tested." (Clode's Military and Martial Law, 2d ed., p. 55.) In 1788 "A Collection of Regulations and Orders" was issued, and this seems to have been the first authoritative issue of such a system. The war office regulations were collected and issued in 1807, and the "General Regulations and Orders for the Army, Adjutant General's Office, Horse Guards," in 1811. A collection of army regulations by Thomas Simes was published in 1772, under the title, "The Military Guide for Young Officers," but this publication had no official sanction.

By the term "system of army regulations" is meant an authorized publication, such as our Army Regulations, consisting of general rules, made by the executive authority, for the government, interior economy, and instruction of the army, and the administration of its affairs. The most noted executive regulations of the British military service, which, within a less comprehensive, but most important field, were indeed a very complete system, were the Articles of War, which, before the enactment of the army discipline act of 1879, constituted, together with the mutiny act, the code of discipline by which the British army was governed. The sovereign still has (under the Army Act) power to make Articles of War, but, owing to the elaborateness of the statutory code, it is regarded as improbable that the exercise of this power, for the purpose of prescribing the punishments for

and if it were practicable for Congress completely to regulate the methods of military administration, it might, under the Constitution, do so. But it is military offences, will ever again be necessary. For a short, but very good, sketch of the history of this law-making by prerogative and by executive regulation authorized by statute, see Encyclopedia Britannica, title "Military Law." In 1686 a work entitled "An Abridgment of the English Military Discipline" was published. It consisted principally of drill regulations, but also related to encamping, garrisons, guards, and "councels of war or courts-martial." Some interesting regulations of the time of Queen Anne, recently discovered in the record office of the British Museum, are published in the Journal of the Military Service Institution for November, 1897.

The Rules of Procedure are authorized by the Army Act, in the following terms:

"1. Subject to the provisions of this act Her Majesty may, by rules to be signified under the hand of a secretary of state, from time to time make, and when made repeal, alter, or add to, provisions in respect of the following matters or any of them; that is to say,

(a) The assembly and procedure of courts of inquiry;
(b) The convening and constituting of courts-martial;
(c) The adjournment, dissolution, and sittings of courts-martial;
(d) The procedure to be observed in trials by court-martial;
(e) The confirmation and revision of the findings and sentences of courts-martial; and enabling the authority having power under section 57 of this act to commute sentences to substitute a valid sentence for an invalid sentence of a court-martial;
(f) The carrying into effect sentences of courts-martial;
(g) The forms of orders to be made under the provisions of this act relating to courts-martial, penal servitude, or imprisonment;
(h) Any matter in this act directed to be prescribed;
(i) Any other matter or thing expedient or necessary for the purpose of carrying this act into execution so far as relates to the investigation, trial, and punishment of offenses triable or punishable by military law;

"2. Provided always, that no such rules shall contain anything contrary to or inconsistent with the provisions of this act.

"3. All rules made in pursuance of this section shall be judicially noticed.

"4. All rules made in pursuance of this section shall be laid before Parliament as soon as practicable after they are made, if Parliament be then sitting, and if Parliament be not then sitting, as soon as practicable after the beginning of the then next session of Parliament."

entirely impracticable, and therefore it is in a great measure left to the President to do it. So far as Congress chooses to exercise its jurisdiction in this respect it occupies the field, and the President can not encroach on it.[1] But when it does not see fit to do so, the President's power is of necessity called into action. It is, indeed, of the commonest occurrence for Congress to regulate a subject in part and for the Executive to regulate some remaining part, and this without any pretense of statutory authority, but upon the broad basis of constitutional power. We thus have a legislative jurisdiction and, subject to it, an executive jurisdiction extending over the same matter.[2] It could not be otherwise. Congress can not regulate all the details for the execution of all the laws, and the authority charged with their execution must therefore come to its aid.[3]

---

[1] 2 Opin. Atty. Gen., 231; 6 id., 10, 215.

[2] The War Department has recognized this by its approval of the following views: "The issue of duplicate discharges, or certificates in lieu of lost discharges, is a matter over which both Congress and the President have control, the former by virtue of the power 'to make rules for the government and regulation of the land and naval forces,' and the latter by virtue of his power as Executive and Commander in Chief. The power of Congress is, however, the superior power, and therefore nothing in conflict with any regulation on the subject made by Congress can legally be prescribed by the President, but the fact that Congress has made a regulation partly covering the subject does not take away from the President his power to make a regulation relating to the part not covered."

[3] Winthrop's Military Law, p. 20, note:

"If it is difficult," says Judge Cooley, "to point out the precise boundary which separates legislative from judicial duties, it is still more difficult to discriminate, in particular cases, between what is properly legislative and what is properly executive duty. The authority that makes the laws has large discretion in determining the means through which they shall be executed; and the performance of many duties which they may provide for by law they may refer either to the chief executive of the State, or,

So, also, as between the legislative and judicial powers, Congress may regulate the procedure of the Federal courts, but in so far as it does not do it the courts may prescribe their own regulations. And this is in fact the existing condition. Congress has exercised the power in part, leaving it to the courts to regulate what it has not provided for. Courts can not exercise their jurisdiction without rules of procedure, and necessarily have the original power of adopting their own when the legislature does not prescribe them; just as the President can not exercise

at their option, to any other executive or ministerial officer, or even to a person specially named for the duty. What can be definitely said on this subject is this: That such powers as are specially conferred by the constitution upon the governor, or upon any other specified officer, the legislature can not require or authorize to be performed by any other officer or authority; and from those duties which the constitution requires of him he can not be excused by law. But other powers or duties the executive can not exercise or assume except by legislative authority, and the power which in its discretion it confers it may also in its discretion withhold, or confide to other hands. Whether in those cases where power is given by the constitution to the governor, the legislature have the same authority to make rules for the exercise of the power that they have to make rules to govern the proceedings in the courts, may perhaps be a question. It would seem that this must depend generally upon the nature of the power, and upon the question whether the constitution, in conferring it, has furnished a sufficient rule for its exercise. Where complete power to pardon is conferred upon the executive, it may be doubted if the legislature can impose restrictions under the name of rules or regulations; but where the governor is made commander in chief of the military forces of the State, it is obvious that his authority must be exercised under such proper rules as the legislature may prescribe, because the military forces are themselves under the control of the legislature, and military law is prescribed by that department. There would be this clear limitation upon the power of the legislature to prescribe rules for the executive department: that they must not be such as, under pretense of regulation, divest the executive of, or preclude his exercising, any of his constitutional prerogatives or powers. Those matters which the constitution specifically confides to him the legislature can not directly or indirectly take from his control." (Cooley's Constitutional Limitations, p. 133.)

his power as commander-in-chief without the power to make orders for the regulation of the Army. In fact, each branch of the Government—the legislative, executive, and judicial—has the original power of making regulations for the transaction of its business—most manifestly so when the business is of direct constitutional origin—but the legislative has sometimes a jurisdiction over the regulations of the other branches, and when this happens its jurisdiction is superior.[1]

In speaking of the power of Congress over the administration of the affairs of the Army, it is, of course, not intended to include what would properly come under the head of the direction of military movements.[2] This belongs to command, and neither the power of Congress to raise and support armies, nor the power to make rules for the government and regulation of the land and naval forces, nor the power to declare war, gives it the command of the Army. Here the constitutional power of the President as commander-in-chief is exclusive.

When Congress fails to make regulations with reference to a matter of military administration, but either expressly or silently leaves it to the President to do it, it does not delegate its own legislative power to him, because that would be unconstitutional,[3] but expressly

[1] Under the Constitution, each house of Congress determines its own rules of proceedings.

[2] Fleming v. Page, 9 How., 615.

[3] In McCall's Case (2 Philad., 269), the court said: "Of course Congress can not constitutionally delegate to the President legislative powers; but it may, in conferring powers constitutionally exercisable by him, prescribe, or omit prescribing, special rules of their administration, or may specially authorize him to make the rules. When Congress neither prescribes them, nor expressly

or silently gives him the opportunity to call his executive power into play. It is perhaps not easy to explain why, if regulations may, under the Constitution, be made both by the legislative and executive branches, one should have precedence over the other; but it is to be noticed that the power of Congress is the express one "to make rules for the government and regulation of the land and naval forces," whereas the power of the President is a construction of his position as Executive and Commander-in-Chief. The legislative power, by the words quoted, covers the whole field of military administration, but it is not always certain how far the executive power may go. It is not as well defined as the legislative power, but it is undoubtedly limited to so much of the subject as is not already con-

---

authorizes him to make them, he has the authority, inherent in the powers conferred, of making regulations necessarily incidental to their exercise, and of choosing between legitimate alternative modes of their exercise. Whether his authority extends further, and enables him, without express authority from Congress, to make regulations which, though incidental, are not necessarily so, is a different question. When, however, Congress, in conferring a power which it may constitutionally vest in him, not only omits to prescribe regulations of its exercise, but, as in the present case, expressly authorizes him to make them, he may, within the limits of, and consistently with, the legislative power declared, make any such regulations incidental, though not necessarily so, to the power conferred, as Congress might have specially prescribed."

"When statutes confer powers, impose duties, and provide for the accomplishment of various objects, they are necessarily couched in general terms, but they carry with them, by implication, all the powers, duties, and exemptions necessary to accomplish the objects thereby sought to be attained." (*In re* Neagle, 39 Fed. Rep., 834.)

"The difference between the departments undoubtedly is that the legislature makes, the executive executes, and the judiciary construes the law; but the maker of the law may commit something to the discretion of the other departments, and the precise boundary of this power is a subject of delicate and difficult inquiry, into which a court will not enter unnecessarily." (Wayman *v.* Southard, 10 W., 46 (Marshall, C. J.).)

trolled by the latter.¹ The jurisdiction of the executive power is not, however, within this limit coextensive with that of the legislative power, because the legislative branch of the Government has a constitutional field of operation peculiar to itself, and yet there are army regulations which seem to be of a legislative character. It is because of this that difficulty sometimes occurs—a difficulty which has in the past quite often taken the form of a difference of views between the War Department and the accounting officers of the Treasury.

---

¹ See opinion of Attorney General Wirt, 1 Opin., 549; of Attorney General Berrien, 2 Opin., 225, and of Attorney General Cushing, 6 Opin., 10, 15. "The authority of the Secretary to issue orders, regulations, and instructions, with the approval of the President, in reference to matters connected with the naval establishment, is subject to the condition, necessarily implied, that they must be consistent with the statutes which have been enacted by Congress in reference to the Navy. He may, with the approval of the President, establish regulations in execution of, or supplementary to, but not in conflict with, the statutes defining his powers or conferring rights upon others. The contrary has never been held by this court. What we now say is entirely consistent with Gratiot *v.* United States, 4 How., 80, and *Ex parte* Reed, 100 U. S., 13, upon which the Government relies. Referring in the first case to certain army regulations, and in the other to certain navy regulations, which had been approved by Congress, the court observed that they had the force of law. See also Smith *v.* Whitney, 116 U. S., 181. In neither case, however, was it held that such regulations, when in conflict with the acts of Congress, could be upheld." (United States *v.* Symonds, 120 U. S., 46–49.) And see Winthrop's Military Law, pp. 29, 30, and note; and Dig. Opin. J. A. G., p. 168, § 6.

CHAPTER II.

EXECUTIVE REGULATIONS IN GENERAL.

Before further considering the regulations relating to one branch—the military branch—of the public service, it will perhaps not be uninstructive briefly to examine the subject of executive orders and regulations in general.[1] There is an important distinction which should be kept in mind in this connection, namely, the distinction between offices created by statute and those created by the Constitution. As to the former, the extent of their authority and the manner of its exercise are subject to the control of the legislative branch; but as to an office created by the Constitution, and whose general powers are named in it, and which is not by the Constitution made dependent on legislation for its jurisdiction, its authority can not, as to these constitutional powers, be thus controlled, except in so far as the legislative branch may refuse to vote the means or furnish the opportunity necessary for their exercise, or unless the Constitution itself vests the legislative branch with a superior authority as to some subject-matter over which both it and the executive or judicial branch have jurisdiction. When Congress, by its exercise of the legislative power, creates new subjects of political action, it may, for the execution of the laws relating to them, vest the President with

[1] See article on "Executive Regulations" in the American Law Review, November-December, 1897.

new powers; but where the President is vested with a distinct power by the Constitution, Congress can not control it otherwise than as indicated.[1]

In the Neagle case the United States Circuit Court (39 Fed. Rep., 833) said: "The power and duty imposed on the President to 'take care that the laws are faithfully executed,' necessarily carries with it all power and authority necessary to accomplish the object sought to be attained." And on the appeal of this case the Supreme Court (135 U. S., 63) said: "The Constitution, section 3, Article II, declares that the President 'shall take care that the laws be faithfully executed,' and he is provided with the means of fulfilling this obligation by his authority to commission all the officers of the United States, and, by and with the advice and consent of the Senate, to appoint the

---

[1] "The theory of the Constitution undoubtedly is, that the great powers of the Government are divided into separate departments; and so far as these powers are derived from the Constitution, the departments may be regarded as independent of each other. But beyond that, all are subject to regulations by law, touching the discharge of the duties required to be performed.

"The executive power is vested in a President; and as far as his powers are derived from the Constitution, he is beyond the reach of any other department, except in the mode prescribed by the Constitution through the impeaching power. But it by no means follows, that every officer in every branch of that department is under the exclusive direction of the President. Such a principle, we apprehend, is not, and certainly can not be claimed by the President.

"There are certain political duties imposed upon many officers in the executive department, the discharge of which is under the direction of the President. But it would be an alarming doctrine, that Congress can not impose upon any executive officer any duty they may think proper, which is not repugnant to any rights secured and protected by the Constitution; and in such cases, the duty and responsibility grow out of and are subject to the control of the law, and not to the direction of the President. And this is emphatically the case, where the duty enjoined is of a mere ministerial character." (Kendall v. United States, 12 Pet., 610.)

most important of them and to fill vacancies. He is declared to be commander-in-chief of the army and navy of the United States. The duties which are thus imposed upon him he is further enabled to perform by the recognition in the Constitution, and the creation by acts of Congress, of executive departments, which have varied in number from four or five to seven or eight, the heads of which are familiarly called cabinet ministers. These aid him in the performance of the great duties of his office, and represent him in a thousand acts to which it can hardly be supposed his personal attention is called, and thus he is enabled to fulfill the duty of his great department, expressed in the phrase that 'he shall take care that the laws be faithfully executed.'

"Is this duty limited to the enforcement of acts of Congress or of treaties of the United States according to their *express terms*, or does it include the rights, duties, and obligations growing out of the Constitution itself, our international relations, and all the protection implied by the nature of the Government under the Constitution?"

And the court, Mr. Justice Miller delivering the opinion, then give a number of examples of proper occasions for the exercise of this executive power, and conclude that, while there is no express statute authorizing the appointment of a deputy marshal, or any other officer to attend a judge of the Supreme Court when traveling in his circuit, and to protect him against assaults or other injury, the general obligation imposed upon the President of the United States by the Constitution to take care that the laws are faithfully executed, and the means placed in his hands, both by the Constitution and the laws of the United States, to enable him to do this, impose upon the executive department the duty of protecting a justice or judge of any of the courts of the United States, when there is just reason to believe that he will be in personal danger while executing the duties of his office.

In Wilcox *v.* Jackson, 13 Pet., 498, the Supreme Court held that the President could legally set aside public lands for a military post or Indian agency, in the execution of laws authorizing him to establish them at such places as he might deem best, but not expressly authorizing him to reserve public lands. And in Grisar *v.* McDowell, 6 Wall., 381, the same court call attention to the fact that from an early period in the history of the Government it had been the practice of the President to order, from time to time, as the exigencies of the public service required, parcels of land belonging to the United States to be reserved from sale and set apart for public uses, his authority in this respect being recognized in numerous acts of Congress. Thus, in the Preemption Act of May 29, 1830, it was provided that the right of preemption contemplated by the act should not "extend to any land which is reserved from sale by act of Congress, or *by order of the President,* or which may have been appropriated for any purpose whatever." Again, in the Preemption Act of September 14, 1841, "lands included in any reservation by any treaty, law, *or proclamation of the President,* or reserved for salines or other purpose," were exempted from entry. So by an act of March 3, 1853, it was declared that all public lands in California should be subject to preemption, and offered at public sale, with the exception, among others, "of lands *reserved by competent authority,*" and the court say that by "competent authority" was meant the authority of the President and officers acting under his direction. As to the reservations then in question the court say that they were indirectly approved by the legislation of Congress in appropriating moneys for the construction of fortifications and other public works upon them. And in the case of Swaim *v.* United States,[1] it has been finally settled that the President, as commander-in-chief, has the constitutional power to convene courts-martial—a striking illustration of an undefined constitutional power, for it is nothing less than the power to constitute tribunals with judicial jurisdiction extending even to trials for capital offences.

The President, said Mr. Cushing, "is limited in the exercise of his powers by the Constitution and the laws; but it does not follow that he must show a statutable provision for everything he does. The Government could not be administered upon such a contracted principle. The great outlines of the movements of the Executive may be marked out, and limitations imposed upon the exercise of his powers, yet there are numberless things which must be done, which can not be anticipated and defined, and are essential to useful and healthy action of government.[2]

---

[1] 165 U. S., 553.
[2] 6 Opin. Atty. Gen., 10, 365; 8 *id.*, 343; 10 *id.*, 413. See also Appendixes A and B.

In United States *v.* Macdaniel, 7 Pet., 14, the Supreme Court said: "A practical knowledge of the action of any one of the great departments of the Government, must convince every person that the head of a department, in the distribution of its duties and responsibilities, is often compelled to exercise his discretion. He is limited in the exercise of his powers by the law; but it does

It is well established that "the Secretary of War is the regular constitutional organ of the President for the administration of the military establishment of the nation; and rules and orders publicly promulged through him must be received as the acts of the Executive, and as such, be binding upon all within the sphere of his legal and constitutional authority."[1]

not follow that he must show a statutory provision for every thing he does. No government could be administered on such principles. To attempt to regulate, by law, the minute movements of every part of the complicated machinery of government would evince a most unpardonable ignorance on the subject. Whilst the great outlines of its movements may be marked out, and limitations imposed on the exercise of its powers, there are numberless things which must be done, that can neither be anticipated nor defined, and which are essential to the proper action of the Government. Hence, of necessity, usages have been established in every department of the Government, which have become a kind of common law, and regulate the rights and duties of those who act within their respective limits. And no change of such usages can have a retrospective effect, but must be limited to the future."

In Caha v. United States, 152 U. S., 211, the Supreme Court, through Justice Brewer, said: "The rules and regulations prescribed by the Interior Department in respect to contests before the Land Office were not formally offered in evidence, and it is claimed that this omission is fatal, and that a verdict should have been instructed for the defendant. But we are of opinion that there was no necessity for a formal introduction in evidence of such rules and regulations. They are matters of which courts of the United States take judicial notice. Questions of a kindred nature have been frequently presented, and it may be laid down as a general rule, deducible from the cases, that wherever, by the express language of any act of Congress, power is intrusted to either of the principal departments of Government to prescribe rules and regulations for the transaction of business in which the public is interested, and in respect to which they have a right to participate, and by which they are to be controlled, the rules and regulations prescribed in pursuance of such authority become a mass of that body of public records of which the courts take judicial notice."

[1] United States v. Eliason, 16 Pet., 302; United States v. Fletcher, 148 U. S., 84; Opinion of Attorney General Cushing, 7 Opin., 453. The latter is an especially full and interesting discussion of this point.

So that if section 161 of the Revised Statutes, above mentioned, can be said to have any reference to the administration of military affairs, it would seem to be to this extent unnecessary, the President already having the constitutional authority to prescribe regulations for this purpose through the Secretary of War.[1] An act of Congress, professedly conferring on the President the power to do an act which he already may do by virtue of his constitutional authority, is no more than a declaration of the existing power. But the Secretary of War does not hold an office created and defined by the Constitution. His office is a statutory one, and its authority is subject to the control of Congress, except in so far as his acts are acts of the President, in the exercise of a constitutional function, in a matter over which Congress has not a superior constitutional power. Therefore, section 161 of the Revised Statutes may be regarded as conferring the authority described directly on him as one of the heads of departments referred to, and this is not to be regarded as a delegation of legislative power; a distinction, although not a well-defined one, existing between those important subjects which must be entirely regulated by Congress and those of less interest, in reference to which a general provision is made and power is given to those who may act under it to fill up the details as incidental to its execution. This matter is fully discussed in Griner's case, 16 Wis., 447.[2] But the regulations which the Secretary of War is thus empowered to make are purely depart-

---

[1] 6 Dec. First Comptroller, 13.
[2] See also United States v. Webster, 2 Ware, 16; 28 Fed. Cases, 515, 517.

mental regulations for the transaction of the departmental business of the War Department. They are not Army regulations proper.

Regulations made pursuant to, or in execution of, statutes are very common. (See title "Regulations," in the index of the Revised Statutes; and see the opinion of Mr. J. M. Dickinson, Acting Attorney General, dated October 24, 1896, *Appendix C*.)

In the case of the United States *v.* Breen[1] the constitutionality of such regulations, made pursuant to legislation declaring any violation of them a misdemeanor and punishable by fine and imprisonment, was fully recognized. In that case Mr. Justice Lamar said:

"The only ground relied upon in behalf of the defendant is, that the authority conferred by the act of Congress on the Secretary of War to make and promulgate said rules and regulations is legislative, and can not, under the Constitution of the United States, be, by act of Congress, conferred upon the Secretary of War or anyone else, so as to make a violation thereof a crime against the United States. Whether this is so or not is the only question to be determined.

"If the law empowered the Secretary of War, by rule or regulation, to make a certain act criminal, and punishable as such, then this prosecution would not be maintainable; but it is not the rule and regulation which declares the violation thereof a crime, and punishable. All that the Secretary is authorized to do is to make the rule and regulation. It is the act of Congress which declares that the unlawful and willful violation of such rule and regulation, after it is pro-

---

[1] 10 Fed. Rep. 102.

mulgated, shall be held a misdemeanor by the person violating the same, and that such person shall be sentenced to pay a fine not exceeding $500, and shall suffer imprisonment not exceeding six months as a penalty therefor. Numerous acts of Congress have been passed authorizing the Postmaster General, and other members of the executive department, to make rules and regulations for the business pertaining to their respective departments, and declaring that, when made and promulgated, a willful and unlawful violation of them should be held a crime against the United States, and the violators punished as prescribed in the act. The Supreme Court of the United States is authorized by act of Congress to adopt certain rules for the government of the inferior courts, which, when made, have the force and effect of law as much as if such rules were directly enacted by Congress, and approved by the President. The same effect is to be given to the rule and regulation made by the Secretary in this case. The act of Congress denounces the violation of it as a crime, and prescribes the penalty. The criminality of the violation of the rule, and the liability of the offender to indictment and to punishment upon trial and conviction, result directly and exclusively from the legislation of Congress."[1]

[1] In Woods v. Gary, Mr. Justice Cox of the supreme court of the District of Columbia, said:

"If an act of Congress, presumed to be approved by the President, vests in the judges or heads of the departments authority to appoint subordinate officers, then, by constitutional authority, the power to appoint them is taken away from the President; and it follows, according to this case, that the power of removal would be equally taken away. The President might dismiss the head of a department who would refuse at his request to dismiss a subordinate or inferior officer, but would have no power directly to dismiss such officer himself.

"It may be regarded, then, as the settled law that the power of removal is incident to the power of appointment, and, therefore, that any law which confers upon the head of a department a power of appointment, ipso facto, conveys a power of removal, as effectually as if that power were expressly given by the statute. The power of removal is intrenched in the law. It is created by an act of legislation, and it can only be taken away or modified by similar authority. The acts of Congress, therefore, authorizing the appointment of complainant as inspector of mails, of themselves gave the Postmaster General authority to remove him at pleasure, unless that or some other act of Congress has imposed some limitation, condition, or restriction upon that power.

"And this brings us to the inquiry whether and how far, if at all, the act of January 16, 1883, commonly known as the Civil Service Act, affects the power of removal at pleasure which the Postmaster General would possess under his general authority to appoint this class of officers. It does, indeed, very materially modify the power of appointment theretofore existing, but it does not purport to affect the power of removal, except in a single particular.

"In section 13 it provides that: 'No officer or employee of the United States mentioned in this act shall discharge or promote or degrade, or in any manner change the official rank or compensation of any other officer or employee, or promise or threaten to do so, for giving or withholding or neglecting to make any contribution of money or other valuable thing for any political purpose.'

"Substantially the same is directed to be provided by rules, to be established by the Commission and the President, in clause 3 of the second section. In no other single respect is the power of removal affected by any substantive and direct enactment of this law.

"But it is claimed that the Commission is empowered to prepare rules in aid of the President for carrying this act into effect, and that said rules, when prepared and promulgated, have the force and effect of law, and that such effect is to be given to the rules under which the complainant seeks relief.

"There can be no doubt as to the power of Congress or any other legislative body to delegate to subordinate authorities the power to make rules and regulations within certain limits, which, when made, will have the force of law. Thus, corporations, municipal or private, may be authorized to make by-laws, and police commissioners, boards of health, and fire commissioners may be authorized to make regulations which have the effect of laws.

"But if any rule prepared by this Commission, whether published by the President or not, should have the effect of repealing or modifying an act of Congress, it would be an act of legislation, and not a regulation of a mere executive character, which it was clearly the object of this law to authorize. It is a grave question whether Congress could delegate to the President, or to any board of commissioners, jointly with the President, the authority to do any act which is equivalent to legislation.

"I am not aware that the Supreme Court has made any delivery upon this question, but there is a uniform current of authorities in the State courts against the power of any legislature so to delegate their authority. See the authorities collected in the American and English Encyclopedia of Law, volume 3, page 698, under the proposition:

"'It is an established proposition of constitutional law that the power conferred upon the legislature to enact laws cannot be delegated by that department to any other body or authority.'

"One illustration was the case of a statute of Minnesota which left it to certain judges to decide whether a law should be submitted to the people (State v. Young, 29 Minn., 474), and another was a law which conferred upon the district court the power to incorporate towns (People v. Nevada, 6 Cal., 143; State v. Simons, 32 Minn., 540); both of which forms of legislation were held unconstitutional.

"But probably all courts would agree that no law is to be construed so as to amount to a delegation of legislative authority that can be avoided. An illustration of this rule is found in the case of Interstate Commerce Commission v. Railway Company, 167 U. S., 479. The Interstate Commerce Act required that all charges on railroads should be reasonable and just, and every other was declared to be unlawful. It prohibited discrimination, undue preferences, etc. It created the Interstate Commerce Commission, gave it authority to inquire into the management and business of all common carriers, and added: 'And the Commission is hereby authorized to execute and enforce the provisions of this act.'

"Under this authority, the Interstate Commerce Commission undertook, by an order, to establish a schedule of rates for certain railroad companies, and, upon the refusal of the latter to observe them, applied to the circuit court for the southern district of Ohio for a mandamus to enforce their order, and, this being refused, appealed to the court of appeals, and the latter court certified to the Supreme Court of the United States the question whether the Commission had the jurisdictional power to make the order before mentioned. Justice Brewer, in delivering the opinion of the court in the negative, said, in construing the act of Congress: 'The power given is the power to execute and enforce, not to legislate. The power is partly judicial, partly executive and administrative, but not legislative.'"

"Again:

"'We have, therefore, these considerations presented: First. The power to prescribe a tariff of rates for carriage by a common carrier is a legislative and not an administrative or judicial function, and, having respect to the large amount of property invested in railroads, the various companies engaged therein, the thousands of miles of road, and the millions of tons of freight carried, the varying and diverse conditions attaching to such carriage, is a power of supreme delicacy and importance. Second. That Congress has transferred such a power to any administrative body is not to be presumed or implied from any doubtful and uncertain language. The words and phrases efficacious to make such a delegation of power are well understood and have been frequently used, and if Congress had intended to grant such a power to the Interstate Commerce Commission it can not be doubted that it would have used language open to no misconstruction, but clear and direct. Third. Incorporating into a statute the common law obligation resting upon the carrier to make all its charges reasonable and just, and directing the Commission to execute and enforce the provisions of the act, does not by implication carry to the Commission or invest it with the power to exercise the legislative function of prescribing rates which shall control in the future.'

"And so, with equal emphasis, it may be said that the authority to the Civil Service Commission to aid the President in preparing rules for carrying the act creating that Commission into effect, does not by implication confer upon the President a right to virtually repeal an existing law, especially when, as we shall see, that is not at all necessary to the effectual operation of the act itself. And lastly, there is nothing in the language of the act or the objects which it professes to attain which make it necessary to attribute such executive power to the Commission or the President. The act nowhere requires that the power of removal vested in the head of a department shall be abridged except in the single particular of removal, because of the refusal to contribute for partisan purposes; and therefore it is not necessary, in order to carry the act into effect, that any rule should be adopted abridging the power of removal of the Postmaster General or other head of a department in any other respect.

"The second section contains an enumeration of the objects for which the rules are to provide. They are: For competitive examination, for appointment by selection from those grades highest as the result of such examinations, for apportionment of the appointments among the States and Territories and the District of Columbia, according to population, for a period of probation before absolute appointment, for exemption of persons in the public service from any obligation to contribute to any political fund and from being coerced into any political action, and for noncompetitive examination in certain cases, and for notice to the Commission of all appointments made by the appointing power.

"It would be a very irrational interpretation which would give to the words 'and among other things,' which are prefixed to this enumeration, such a scope of meaning as to convey by implication an unlimited authority to establish rules having no relation to the objects of the law. If that were a proper interpretation of the law, these rules might be made to impose new conditions to the power of appointment, and even take it away from the heads of the departments and vest it in the Commission itself. The absurdity of such a proceeding would be manifest, and yet it would be no more obnoxious to criticism than rules modifying the power of removal, as it existed before the act was passed, or in a manner not warranted by the law itself.

"The law seems to contemplate the preparation of these rules as the joint act of the Commission and the President. It directs that when promulgated they shall be observed by all the officers in the departments. It does not in terms declare by whose authority they are to be promulgated and to go into effect, but it is to be presumed that it is to be by the President. It makes no difference, however, whether they are to emanate from the President or the Commission, for Congress is just as incapable of surrendering its legislative authority to the President as to the Commission; and is just as little to be understood as intending to do so in the one case as in the other. The simple inquiry is whether the rules invoked by the complainant, whether the President or the Commission, or both, be the authors of them, are such as the act of January 16, 1883, known as the Civil Service Act, authorized to be established. In my judgment they are ultra vires and void.

"I have no doubt that the President may lay down rules for the internal policy of his Administration, and may require his chief executive officers, dependent upon his pleasures for their tenure of office, to conform to them, or else to sever their official relations with him, and in that sense the rules relied on by the complainant were within his political and executive authority. But the enforcement of such rules is a matter between the President and his Cabinet, and not a matter for the courts, or one in which the complainant has any legal interest. All that I mean to state in this opinion is that the rules in question were not such as the Civil Service Act authorizes, and do not derive any efficacy from that act.

"I know of nothing more important to the true interests of the country than the policy which the civil-service legislation was intended to initiate and promote, and it is perhaps a matter for great regret that the act of January 16, 1883, has not gone further than it does. But it is my duty to construe it as it is.

"To sum up, I conclude that, apart from the Civil Service Act, the Postmaster General had the authority to remove the complainant from office at his pleasure; that this act makes no change in this respect, except to forbid removals for refusal to contribute to partisan objects; that the power to the Commission and the President to establish rules to carry that act into effect does not authorize any rule which shall make a change in the law in this respect, and that even if this court had jurisdiction in a case like the present, the complainant is not entitled to the relief prayed."

In Carr v. Gordon, 82 Fed. Rep., 379, it was said with reference to a civil service rule:

"But on July 27, 1897, the President of the United States promulgated an order announced as an amendment to rule 11, as follows: 'No removal shall be made from any position subject to competitive examination except for just cause, and upon written charges filed with the head of the department or other appointing officer, and of which the accused shall have full notice, and an opportunity to make defense.' This is an authoritative expression by the Executive of the United States of his desire and command to his subordinates with respect to removal from office of those coming within the scope of the civil service regulations. Possessed by the Constitution of the power of appointment and removal, except, possibly, as he may be therein restricted by act of Congress, the Executive has the right to regulate for himself the manner of appointment and removal. He may direct his subordinates, who exercise under him, in certain cases, the power of appointment and removal, with respect thereto, and may regulate the manner in which they may act for him; but this is an administrative order of the Executive, not made in compliance with any law, or in regulation of the execution of any law enacted by Congress restricting his right of removal, but is simply an instruction to those who hold positions by virtue of his appointment of the manner in which they shall discharge their duties in respect to the removal of their subordinates. The order is not the law of the land; it is not the emanation of the law-making power, but is merely a regulation adopted by the Executive, as he rightfully might, in regulation of the conduct of those who are subject to his authority. He made it, and may, at his pleasure, rescind it. The law of the land is not subject to repeal by the Executive. The regulation and orders of the Executive or heads of departments under authority granted by Congress—such as the order under consideration here—are regulations prescribed by law in the sense that acts done under them are upheld; and in that light they may have the force of law. But the failure to do the act thereby enjoined, or the doing of the act thereby prohibited, does not render one liable to the law. United States v. Eaton, 144 U. S., 677, 688, 12 Sup. Ct., 764. Consequently, no vested right to hold office indefinitely is acquired by the incumbent by virtue of the executive regulation in question. This executive order or regulation, therefore, confers no right upon the incumbent of office of which a court of equity can take cognizance. He who disobeys such order of the President is responsible to, and must be dealt with by, him. Courts of equity are not constituted to regulate the departments of the government.

Their jurisdiction is limited to the protection of the rights of property. They have no concern, as I understand the boundaries of their jurisdiction, over the appointment and removal of public officers."

See also Taylor v. Kercheval, 82 Fed. Rep., 497, in which case the court said: "It needs neither argument nor citation of authority to demonstrate that neither the President nor the Civil Service Commission is clothed with legislative powers. Neither can change the law, either by repeal or by making a new enactment. And it is equally elementary that Congress can not delegate its legislative powers either to the President or the Civil Service Commission. The rules promulgated which place office deputies in the marshal's office in the classified civil list are not a statute, nor have they the force of law. They are merely executive rules and regulations, promulgated by authority of law, and are effective, if at all, only as rules and regulations for the internal control and government of the civil service and the executive departments. The courts of chancery have no jurisdiction or authority to enforce such rules or regulations. Their enforcement lies within the domain of the executive departments, which possess ample power to enforce the proper observance of and subordination to the rules and regulations promulgated by the Executive for the government of those employed in any executive department of the government. If the marshal, by the removal or threatened removal of the complainant, has violated, or is about to violate, those rules and regulations, there is ample power in the Department of Justice to redress the wrong, without any resort to a court of chancery."

But see the case of Butler v. White, 83 Fed. Rep., 578, in which the court held:

"First, that the act known as the 'Civil Service Act,' is constitutional; second, that Congress has not delegated to the President and the Commission legislative powers; third, that by rule 3, sec. 1, the Internal Revenue Service has been placed under the Civil Service Act and rules made in pursuance of it; fourth, that the plaintiffs in these actions are officers of the Government in the Internal Revenue Service; fifth, that they cannot be removed from their positions except for causes other than political, in which even their removal must be made under the terms and provisions of the Civil Service Act and the rules promulgated under it, which, under the act of Congress, became a part of the law; sixth, that the attempt to change the position and rank of the officers in these cases is in violation of law; seventh, that a court of equity has jurisdiction to restrain the appointing power from removing the officers from their positions if such removals are in violation of the Civil Service Act."

But it is not necessary to give further examples of regulations made pursuant to, or in execution of, statutes. They are to be met with throughout our political system, and are a necessary part of its machinery.[1]

The power to make regulations is not, indeed, confined to political bodies or officers. It enters into other relations of life—wherever, in fact, *government* is necessary.[2] (See *post*, page 82, note). Thus, corporations possess the power of making regulations, including by-laws. Social clubs have the power, and their regulations are recognized by the courts as binding.[3] We here speak of by-laws as regulations. In one

---

[1] It would require too much space to enumerate all the statutory provisions of this class down to the present time, in which "regulations," as such, are authorized to be prescribed. For the principal of those enacted prior to 1886, reference may be had to the first edition of this work, page 18–19, note 3. Repeated instances also occur in the statutes where, though the word "regulations" is not employed, the same meaning is conveyed by some equivalent term or expression: as by the term "directions," "instructions," "forms," "requirements," "restrictions," "conditions," "limitations," "by laws." Not unfrequently a thing is required by the statute to be done in such manner, etc., as a head of a department, etc., "may prescribe." The "Regulations for the Government of the Revenue-Cutter Service of the United States," issued by the Secretary of the Treasury, April 4, 1894, and resting on no authority more express than is found in the terms of sections 2758 and 2762, placing this corps (consisting of the officers and crews of thirty-six vessels) under the general direction of the Secretary, is a striking illustration of the discretion exercised by heads of departments in making regulations as to matters of detail. (Winthrop's Military Law and Precedents, p. 18.)

[2] "A regulation is merely a 'governing direction.' It implies authority on one side—subjection on the other. * * * It is distinguished from *contract*, which implies the right of all parties to stipulate for terms. * * * A regulation is an order by authority." (Hon. William Lawrence, 1 Dec. First Comp., 55.)

[3] Every public assembly has the power to make and enforce certain rules for the transaction of business and the preservation of order. (Jameson on Constitutional Conventions, p. 463.) Passenger-carriers may prescribe reasonable regulations for the control of passengers, and employers for their employees.

sense a distinction has been made between them in the law of corporations, the by-law being held to be more usually established for the government of the internal affairs of the corporation, while the regulation is regarded as intended for the government of its business with the public.[1] But the word *regulation* is here used in a broader sense and as including the by-law.

In the case of Yturbide v. The Metropolitan Club, the court of appeals of the District of Columbia said:

"There is no longer any question of the right of a corporation, such as that of the respondent in this case, to make by-laws, even in the absence of express statutory power, and to exercise the power of amotion, as incident to the corporation. This has been regarded as the settled law since the case of Lord Bruce, 2 Strange, 819, and the subsequent exposition of the whole doctrine in the case of Rex v. Richardson, 1 Burr., 517, 539, by Lord Mansfield, speaking for the Court of King's Bench in 1758. In this last mentioned case, after reviewing the former decisions and the previous doctrine upon the subject, and showing that the older cases had maintained a doctrine that had been modified by the more recent cases, the Lord Chief Justice said: 'We all think this modern opinion is right. It is *necessary* to the good order and government of corporate bodies, that there should be such a power (that of amotion), as much as the power to make by-laws. Lord Coke says (Bagg's Case, 11 Co. 98a) 'there is a tacit condition annexed to the franchise which, if he breaks, he may be disfranchised.' But where the offence is merely against his duty as a corporator, he can only be tried for it by the corporation.

---

[1] Thompson on Corporations, sec. 937.

Unless the power is *incident*, franchises or offices might be forfeited for offences, and yet there would be no means to carry the law into execution. Suppose a by-law made to give power of amotion for just cause, such a by-law would be good. If so, a corporation, by virtue of an incidental power, may raise to themselves authority to remove for just cause, though not expressly given by charter or prescription.' The doctrine of that celebrated case has never been questioned from the time it was announced, and it is the law, both in England and in this country, at the present day. Com. v. St. Patrick Ben. Soc., 2 Binn., 448, 449; 2 Kent. Com., 297."

As already stated with reference to Army regulations made pursuant to statute, regulations of this kind may be modified, but exceptions to them in individual cases can not legally be made.¹ There is,

---

¹ This is illustrated by the following newspaper comments (1897):

The appointment of General Tyner to be Assistant Attorney General for the Post Office Department has been criticised by some as a violation of the civil service law, in that the place being under the Post Office Department was included within the classified service by an order of President Cleveland.

Civil Service Commissioner Procter to-day stated that when President Cleveland ordered the classification of the Post Office Department, it was not supposed that the place of Assistant Attorney General for that Department was within the scope of that order. When it was found that such was the case, the matter was brought to the attention of President McKinley, who excepted the place, allowing the appointment to be made without examination by the Civil Service Commission.

The announcement that the President had excepted this place after it had been included in the classified service, even if such classification was the result of a mistake, has created surprise, as the Commission has contended that when once a place was included in the classified service by order of the President, under authority of the civil service law, such action had the force of law and could not be rescinded except by act of Congress.

At the office of the Civil Service Commission to-day it was stated that this view of the effect of once including a place in

however, a difference to be observed in this respect between general regulations and specific acts. Ordinarily when an executive officer is empowered by law to do one specific act, as, for example, to reserve public land for a specific public use, his doing this act exhausts his power as to the subject-matter. So, where he is empowered to do a specific set of acts. But when he is given a general discretionary power to make regulations in execution of a law, the power to modify regulations once made is included in it.

A distinction should, however, be made between essential regulations made in aid of a statute, such as are necessary to the execution of the statute and thus have the appearance of being of a decidedly legislative character, and regulations which are merely supplemental to these and relate to the minor details of the machinery for the execution of the statute. These are, to be sure, made in aid of it also, but are not of the character referred to. It is, however, impossible to lay down any rule which would enable us, at a glance, to distinguish in every case the one from the other. There is not always a clear-cut line of demarcation. The distinction exists, but its application must be controlled by the facts of each case.

The Judge-Advocate General's Office has applied the principle of the binding character of regulations made in execution of statutes to regulations made for the disbursement of an appropriation, holding that when

---

the classified service was the accepted opinion of the Commission, but it was not generally understood that the President still retained the power to "except" any place from examination and to make the appointment without the intervention of the Commission, the place still being in the classified service, the only restriction placed upon such power being the provision that he could make "necessary" exceptions.

Congress makes an appropriation, but leaves it to the Executive to prescribe regulations for its disbursement, such regulations should be regarded as made in execution of a statute (although not actually pursuant to it), and therefore as falling under the rule that they are binding on the authority who made them as well as on others, and that they may be modified, but that individual exceptions to them can not be made. And the action of the War Department is understood to have been a confirmation of this view. The regulations in question related to the expenditure for the transportation of deceased soldiers to the place of burial.[1] Another example of a regulation of this

---

[1] The Judge-Advocate General's views were, on this occasion, stated as follows:

"Paragraph 162, Army Regulations, provides that the remains of deceased soldiers will be transported by the Quartermaster's Department to the nearest military post or National Cemetery for burial, unless the commanding officer deems burial at the place of death proper. It also prescribes that the expense of transporting the remains is payable from the appropriation for Army transportation.

"In the case presented in this communication transportation for the remains of a deceased soldier from Fort Walla Walla to Middletown, Pennsylvania, is asked for, and my opinion is desired as to whether the Secretary of War has authority to grant the request.

"The regulation cited is one for the disbursement of a public fund. The appropriation act does not prescribe regulations for this disbursement, but leaves it to the Executive to do so. This is the same, in effect, as if Congress had expressly authorized the Executive to make regulations. Therefore, regulations made by the Secretary of War, determining the amounts of the disbursements of the appropriation should, it is believed, be regarded as made in aid of a statute. Such parts of the regulation as relate to the purely administrative machinery for the expenditure of the appropriation may, however, in my opinion, be distinguished from the quasi legislative part prescribing the amounts of the disbursements. To the former I have no doubt the Secretary of War can make exceptions; to the latter I am of opinion that he can not. Regulations of this kind should, for the purposes of such inquiry as is made in this case, be classed

kind is that fixing the fees of civilian witnesses before courts-martial, for, although in deference to the views of the Comptroller of the Treasury these fees have been made to conform to those of witnesses before the Federal courts, as regulated by the Revised Statutes, this regulation is none the less an exercise of the executive power in carrying out an appropriation, and has

with those made pursuant to statute, as to which I am of opinion that they should be held to have become a part of the law, and to be of the same force as the statute itself, and that, although they may be changed by the authority making them, they are binding on such authority so long as they are not changed, and that he can not grant exceptions to them. (See my remarks on the Army Regulations, page 4, section 2, *ante*, p. 6.)

"It is true that in cases like the present the regulation is not actually made pursuant to statute. The statute does not itself expressly provide for the making of the regulation, but leaves it to be done by the Executive in the exercise of the constitutional power vested in him as commander-in-chief and by the requirement that he shall 'take care that the laws be faithfully executed.' But the regulation is none the less in aid of the statute, in the relation which I have indicated—prescribing an essential rule for the disbursements to be made under the statute, and not merely relating to the administrative means of applying the rule.

"This seems to me to be the sound view to take of this matter. The action of the War Department has, however, not been consistent with reference to regulations of this class—possibly because the difference between them and purely administrative regulations, having no such intimate relation with statutes, has not been noticed. With reference to the regulations made pursuant to the act of Congress relating to the examination of enlisted men for promotion, it has been held that they can not be waived in individual cases, and, on the other hand, as I am informed, the regulation prescribing the per diem allowances of civilian employees when traveling under orders has been waived in individual cases. (I understand that the right to make this waiver has been recognized by the Comptroller of the Treasury, although in a decision of the Assistant Comptroller with reference to the transportation of officer's baggage the latter seems to recognize the distinction which I have made, for he admits the right of the Secretary of War to make an exception to a regulation prescribing the method of transporting an officer's baggage, while apparently not admitting his right to make an exception increasing the money allowance for it in an individual case.)

no dependence on the statute with which it has been made to conform.¹ And another example of such a

"The practice of the War Department does not therefore appear to be uniform, but, in my opinion, its action in the matter of the regulations made in aid of the statute relating to the promotion of enlisted men is based on the correct view of this question, and, applying what was held in that matter, to the present case, I am of opinion that the exception to a regulation, asked for, would be contrary to the true conception of the force of such regulations and therefore unauthorized."

As to the President's power to make regulations prescribing allowances, see United States v. Webster, 28 Fed. Cases, 509; United States v. Ripley, 7 P., 18; 24 Ct. Cls., 209.

¹ The following is an extract from a report of the Acting Judge-Advocate General, dated February 6, 1893, when this subject was under discussion:

"In the Army Appropriations Act an appropriation is each year made for the 'compensation of reporters and witnesses attending upon courts-martial and courts of inquiry.' No rate of compensation is prescribed, nor is it in terms indicated by whom the rate shall be fixed; but these appropriations have from year to year been made with the knowledge and in recognition of the fact that the law was being supplemented by regulations fixing the rates of compensation. This has been done for many years, and the propriety of such regulations has thus been distinctly recognized by Congress.

"To me it seems to be entirely clear that the appropriation was intended to be expended under rules prescribed by the head of the Department charged with the expenditure, and that the rate of compensation was a matter left to the discretion of the Secretary of War. The Second Comptroller does indeed refer to section 848 of the Revised Statutes as though it might be held to fix the compensation of civilians attending as witnesses before courts-martial, but that section relates entirely to the Federal judiciary, of which courts-martial form no part, and is no more applicable to courts martial than any other provision of the title ('Judiciary') in which it is found.

"The fixing of the rate of compensation has, it seems to me, been purposely left by Congress to the Secretary of War. It has been intrusted to his discretion, and whenever, in the exercise of that discretion, he established a certain rate, that decision is legally conclusive on all. In my opinion the Second Comptroller, in announcing his intention not to allow payments made according to the rates established by the Secretary of War, is exceeding his authority.

"The disallowance of such payments will give much trouble, and yet I can not recommend the recognition of a right on the

regulation was that by which the reward for the apprehension of deserters was regulated, before Congress
part of the Second Comptroller to set aside a regulation made by the Secretary of War in the exercise of a legal discretion."

The power of the President to determine the amount of fees and allowances, for specified services, when an appropriation for them is made, but Congress does not itself determine the rates of such fees and allowances, is beyond all question, and has been recognized by the practice both of Congress and the Executive, as well as in the decisions of the courts. In United States *v.* Webster, 2 Ware, 46; 28 Fed. Cases, 509, Judge Ware, of the United States district court of Maine, held, with reference to an Army regulation making a certain allowance, as follows:

"Nor do I see how it can be overcome but by a direct denial of the authority of the Department to establish any such rule, with respect to extra allowances, by general regulations and orders. It appears to me, that it is fairly within the authority of the War Department, under the sanction of the President, to establish general rules upon this subject, which, when duly promulgated, will be binding on the rights of the officers. It is not contended that an order of the Executive can control an act of the legislature, or deprive a party of a right acquired under the law. But, as has been remarked, the legislation of Congress can never go into all the minute detail of regulation, involved in the complicated service of the Army. Much must unavoidably be left to the discretion of the high officers, who superintend that branch of the public service; and as these matters of detail are left to the regulation of the Department, it seems to me reasonable, when officers are required to perform services which do not fall within the range of their ordinary duties, that it is properly within the discretion of the Department to determine what, and whether any, extra compensation should be allowed for such extra service, taking care that the rule be uniform, and applying in the same way to all similar cases. An authority of this kind seems to me to be clearly implied, in the reasoning of the court in the cases which have been before mentioned. 'The amount of compensation,' says Mr. Justice McLean, 'in the military service, may depend in some degree upon the regulations of the War Department; but such regulations must be uniform, and applicable to all officers under the same circumstances.' (United States *v.* Ripley, 7 Pet. (32 U. S.), 25.) And in still broader terms he says, in the opinion before quoted, 'Hence, of necessity, usages have been established in every Department of the Government, which have become a kind of common law, and regulate the rights and duties of those who act within respective limits; and no change of those usages can have a retrospective effect, but must be limited to the future.' (United States *v.* McDaniel, *id.*,

was induced to take to itself the determination of the amount of the reward.

It is said that regulations made under a statute may be referred to as a practical interpretation of the statute.[1] In executing the laws it is often necessary for executive officers to interpret and construe them, and this may be done by means of regulations. Such regulations are valid and binding, unless declared by the courts to be erroneous interpretations of the law. Each new tariff act, for example, necessitates many such regulations, and we have a good illustration of this in the Treasury Circular of September 4, 1897, with reference to the entry of personal effects under the act of July 24, 1897. In this circular we find the following definition of the phrase, "residents of the United States returning from abroad," as it occurs in the act:

"The proviso in paragraph 697 contains special provisions and limitations concerning residents of the United States returning from abroad. It therefore

---

15.) If usage is to govern, in what manner does usage become established? Obviously in no other way than by the practice of the Department. Apply the remark to the case now in judgment. A usage of allowing extra pay, for extra services of any particular kind, is established, by its being charged in various instances, and allowed and ordered to be paid, by the Department. It is obvious, therefore, that no usage can be established but by the concurrence of the Department; for no number of charges, however numerous, on the part of the officers, can ever constitute a usage, under which any right can be claimed, unless they have been allowed. It is the allowance which constitutes the usage."

This case was carried to the circuit court by writ of error, but did not come to a hearing until after the decision in the case of United States v. Eliason, 16 Pet. (41 U. S.), 291, made in 1842. It was then affirmed, without argument, upon the authority of that decision.

[1] United States v. Cottingham, 1 Rob. (Va.), 635; Winthrop, 19, note.

becomes necessary to define the term 'residents of the United States returning from abroad,' in order that customs officers may have a reasonable guide in the practical application of the proviso. The word 'resident' has, in law, more than one meaning, much depending upon the connection and purpose in which it is used. As used in this proviso to paragraph 697, it is held by the Department to include all persons leaving the United States and making a journey abroad, and, during their absence, having no fixed place of abode. Persons who have been abroad two years or more, and who have had, during that time, a fixed place of abode for one year or more, will be considered as nonresidents within the meaning of this law."

So, Article 243 of the Naval Regulations of 1896 prescribes as follows: "The title 'commander-in-chief,' when occurring in naval laws, regulations, and other documents, shall be held to refer to the officer in chief command of a fleet or squadron." And the United States circuit court, district of Massachusetts (Colt, J.), recognized this regulation as conclusive, *in re* Jesse G. Grain, December 31, 1897.

And so it is in all the Executive Departments. In making regulations to carry out a statute it is often necessary to place some express interpretation on it; and this interpretation holds good until judicially reversed. But, of course, great care should be taken to avoid strained interpretations.

Many systems of regulations, besides Army and Navy regulations, have been issued, for the transaction of the business of different branches of the Government, such as the postal, patent office, pension office, land office, Indian office, civil service, customs, internal revenue, revenue-cutter service,[1] and other treasury and consular regulations, etc. But these systems of regulations, as they are here called, form by no means the whole of that mass of regulation law which constitutes so large and important a part of our administrative law. All regulations are not

---

[1] The regulations for the government of the Revenue-Cutter Service are in one respect unique; they establish a penal system, including a code of penalties and a system of procedure. No other regulations have ever undertaken to go to this extreme, and it may well be doubted whether the executive power can legally be carried so far. An extract from these regulations is given in Appendix D.

The regulations of the United States Military Academy do, indeed, also prescribe a system of punishments, certain of which may be imposed by the Superintendent, without the intervention of any trial court, but these are regulations for the control of a school, and stand in this respect on a different footing from the regulations for the government of the Revenue-Cutter Service. Moreover they are substantially based on statute, except, more particularly, in those respects in which the authority for the regulations adopted is the power to prescribe the necessary rules for a public institution peopled with persons whom it is necessary to govern and control. They are issued by authority of the President, but, had none been so issued, the Superintendent himself would have had the power to make such reasonable regulations for the government and maintenance of the discipline of the institution as would not be inconsistent with statute or regulations emanating from a higher source, and he now actually has the power as to matters necessary to regulate but which have not been covered by prescribed regulations.

The Superintendent of the Naval Academy has a very comprehensive authority in this respect, which is expressly delegated to him by the Secretary of the Navy. In the exercise of this authority he issues a complete system of "Regulations for the Interior Discipline and Government of the U. S. Naval Academy," covering subjects which, at the Military Academy, are governed by regulations "adopted by the President." Both of these Superintendents, in addition to being in control of schools, are commanding officers of posts, with the authority appertaining to them in that capacity.

See note, page 82.

The regulations for the government of the Revenue-Cutter Service are issued in the exercise of the general executive power of the President, whereas his power to make army regulations

collected together in systems or groups, but an enormous mass of them consists of individual regulations, the knowledge of whose existence even is ordinarily limited to the few who have to apply them to the subjects to which they relate.

It is difficult to form a true conception of the vastness and importance of all this great body of executive regulation law, controlling, as it does, the administration of all the executive departments with its rules of action. And when we consider that these rules of action are in general made, construed, and applied by the same authority, thus combining quasi-legislative, quasi-judicial, and executive action, we cannot fail to be very much impressed with the extent of the jurisdiction covered by them.

In what has been said only the regulation law of the federal government has been considered. When we examine the State systems we find there also a great deal of regulation law—not in such large masses, nor in general of such importance as the federal regulation law, but nevertheless occupying no insignificant place in the State systems.¹ The whole subject is one

---

not based on legislation is derived from his constitutional authority as commander-in-chief. How far this power would extend were Congress not vested with a superior power over the subject, or if, being so vested, it should entirely fail to exercise the power and to provide any system of government for the Army, it would be difficult to estimate. Would he have a power already exercised, with apparently less authorization, in the promulgation of regulations for the government of the Revenue-Cutter Service?

¹ In many of the States the governors have express statutory authority to make regulations for the government of the militia, as, for example, in New Hampshire, where "The commander in chief is authorized to establish and prescribe such rules, regulations, forms, and precedents as he may deem proper, for the use, government, and instruction of the New Hampshire National Guard," and "to make such changes and alterations in

of exceptional interest, and offers an enormous field for investigation.

The Supreme Court has repeatedly recognized the legality and force of Army regulations:

"The Army regulations, when sanctioned by the President, have the force of law, because it is done by him by the authority of law. The regulations of 1825, then, were as conclusive upon the accounting officer of the Treasury, whilst they continued in force, as those of 1836 afterwards were, and as those of 1841 now are. When, then, an officer presents with his account, an authentic document or certificate of his having commanded a post or arsenal, for which an order has been issued from the War Department, in conformity with the provisions of the Army Regulations, allowing double rations, his right to them is established, nor can they be withheld without doing him a wrong, for which the law gives him a remedy." (United States *v.* Freeman, 3 How., 567.)

"As to the Army regulations, this court has too repeatedly said that they have the force of law to make it proper to discuss that point anew." (Gratiot *v.* United States, 4 How., 118.)

---

such rules and regulations from time to time as he may deem expedient; but such rules and regulations shall conform to this act, and to those governing the United States Army, and shall have the same force and effect as the provisions of this act."

In Michigan a "State military board" is created, with power "to prepare and promulgate all articles, rules, and regulations for the government of the State troops, not inconsistent with the laws of the United States, or of this State, and which articles, rules, and regulations, when approved by the commander in chief, shall be in force."

Some of the States have no military regulations of their own, but use the United States Army Regulations, so far as applicable.

"The power of the Executive to establish rules and regulations for the government of the Army is undoubted." (United States v. Eliason, 16 Pet., 301.)

"The Army Regulations derive their force from the power of the President as commander-in-chief, and are binding upon all within the sphere of his legal and constitutional authority." (Kurtz v. Moffitt, 115 U. S., 503.) See also Swaim v. United States, 165 U. S., 553.[1]

With reference to Navy regulations, issued under section 1547 of the Revised Statutes, Attorney General Devens said that what Congress had conferred on the Secretary of the Navy was not any portion of its general power of legislation, but only the right to make appropriate regulations for the performance of their duties by those whom Congress had placed under his official control. But if it is true that the source from which the President derives his authority to make regulations is statutory, in the absence of statute he would have no authority, and this we know not to be so. There is no similar existing provision of law relating to the Army, but the power of the President to make regulations for the Army is unquestioned.

---
[1] See also United States v. Landers, 92 U. S., 77; ex parte Reed, 100 U. S., 13; United States v. Symonds, 120 U. S., 46; and Am. and Eng. Enc. of Law, "Military Law—Army Regulations."

CHAPTER III.

APPROVAL OF REGULATIONS BY CONGRESS.

An impression has existed that a peculiar "force of law" is given to regulations by their approval by Congress, but it seems to be an erroneous one. If, as above stated, the making of regulations is within the jurisdiction both of Congress and the President, but the authority of Congress is superior to that of the President, it follows that when regulations are approved by Congress they can not be altered by him until the approval is removed. To this extent regulations approved by Congress may be said to have a superior force of law to those not thus approved, but this is not the erroneous impression referred to. Precisely what it is, is not clear, but it seems to have been believed that the approval of regulations by Congress makes them of higher obligation. This, however, is not true. Whether approved by Congress or not, they have, so long and so far as they are in force, the force of law,[1] and are therefore binding. The distinction, in this respect, that has sometimes been made between regulations approved by Congress and those not thus approved is misleading.

---

[1] Gratiot v. United States, 4 How., 118; United States v. Barrows, 24 Fed. Cases, 1018; United States v. Wade, 75 Fed. Rep., 261; McCall's Case, 2 Phila., 269; and other authorities cited *ante*, and in Winthrop's Military Law, vol. 1, p. 20, note 2.

Congress has on several occasions given its sanction to Army regulations:

1. An act of March 3, 1813 (2 Stat. L., 819), provided, "That it shall be the duty of the Secretary of the War Department, and he is hereby authorized, to prepare general regulations, better defining and prescribing the respective duties and powers of the several officers in the adjutant general, inspector general, quartermaster general, and commissary of ordnance departments, of the topographical engineers, of the aids of generals, and generally of the general and regimental staff; which regulations, when approved by the President of the United States, shall be respected and obeyed, until altered or revoked by the same authority. And the said general regulations, thus prepared and approved, shall be laid before Congress at their next session."

A system of regulations was laid before Congress, as required by the act. It was published (together with the statutes relating to the military establishment) in book form, from the Adjutant and Inspector General's Office, May 1, 1813, and may also be found in Vol. 1 of the American State Papers on Military Affairs.

2. By act of April 24, 1816 (3 Stat. L., 298), it was prescribed "that the regulations in force before the reduction of the Army be recognized, as far as the same shall be found applicable to the service, subject, however, to such alterations as the Secretary of War may adopt, with the approbation of the President." The reduction referred to was made in June, 1815, pursuant to an act of March 3.

The act of April 24, 1816, did not relate to any particular code of Army Regulations, but to all the regulations which were in force.

3. As stated in some brief remarks on the different editions of Army Regulations, made on a former occasion:

On the 22d December, 1819, the House of Representatives resolved that "the Secretary of War be instructed to cause to be prepared and laid before this House, at the next session of Congress, a system of martial law, and a system of field service and police, for the government of the Army of the United States."

On the 22d December, 1820, the Secretary of War (Calhoun) accordingly submitted a system of "martial law," prepared by Judge-Advocate Major Storrow (which was never adopted), and a system of field service and police, which had been prepared by General Scott, and submitted to the War Department in September, 1818.[1]

---

[1] General Scott, in submitting his code, said:

"I have the honor to inclose, herewith, the analysis of a work long since projected by me. The accomplishment of some similar design seems an important desideratum in our code of military instruction or legislation. But, on this point, the analysis, compared with existing regulations, will best speak for itself. I can only say that the formation of it has cost me much study and reflection, aided by the experience of a ten years' service, in peace and in war, in the line and in the staff, in the infantry and in the artillery.

"When in Europe I collected every work, in French or in English, (not obsolete) on the service, police, discipline, instruction, and administration, of an army. These have been carefully read and collated, and, under the sanction of the War Department, I am now ready to compile a book, to correspond with the several articles of the accompanying analysis; taking, as a basis, our own laws, regulations, orders, and practice, as far as the paucity of the materials may suffice.

"Should the idea of a Board occur, in connection with this offer, I would beg leave to suggest, that, joint labors, of the

December 26, 1820, the Speaker laid them before the House. The document was in manuscript and was ordered to be printed, and a copy laid upon the desk of each member. (It is reprinted in the third volume of the State Papers on Military Affairs.) When the book was printed several copies were sent to General Scott, who made certain corrections, and on the 20th February, 1821, returned a corrected copy (of which he retained a duplicate) to the War Department for the Committee of the House. It was received by the chairman of the Committee on the 23d of February, 1821.

February 27, 1821, the chairman of the Military Committee of the House reported the Senate bill, "To reduce and fix the military peace establishment," with certain amendments, among which was the addition of a section approving and adopting "the system of

---

literary kind, but rarely succeed; and that I have, personally, a repugnance to that sort of employment, which nothing but a positive order could induce me again to forego. Indeed, I am persuaded (and from a personal experience somewhat in point) that, of five individuals, of equal qualifications, either might make a better book than the five taken together."

"Perhaps it might be well to give the titles, etc., of the works from which I should expect to compile; but, as this might also seem ostentatious, without a more apparent necessity, I will, at present, confine myself to the mention of the two following, which are the principal:

"1. 'Législation Militaire, ou recueil méthodique et raisonné des lois, décrets, arrêtés, réglemens et instructions actuellement (1812) en vigueur, sur toutes les branches de l'état militaire,' par Berriat, etc., five large 8vo volumes, pp. 2509. Notwithstanding the title and the bulk of this manual of the French army, it does not contain, except by reference, a syllable of the *tactique* of the several corps.

"2. 'General Regulations and Orders for the Army;' edition of 1813; pp. 326, in 8vo. The British manual, like that above, merely refers to the regulations on tactics. In the execution of the work now proposed, similar references would, occasionally, be necessary."

General Regulations for the Army, compiled by Major-General Scott." The bill, including this (the fourteenth) section, became law *March 2, 1821.* Early in that month, General Scott received directions to put the book to press for the use of the Army, and, having received a letter from the chairman of the Military Committee of the House, informing him that the corrected copy had been received and section 14 added to the Army bill by way of amendment, he caused the book to be reprinted from his retained duplicate corrected copy.

The Regulations were then—July, 1821—issued by the War Department, *with the corrections,* as "formally approved by Congress," except as to fourteen articles, which, it was stated in an order of Secretary of War Calhoun, prefacing the work, had received the sanction of the President.

This gave rise to the question, Was the corrected copy the one approved by Congress? In 1822, a committee of the House of Representatives was appointed to investigate the circumstances attending its publication. Gen. Alexander Smyth, the chairman of the Military Committee, stated that when he proposed section 14, of the act of 1821, to the committee as an amendment, he had reference to the corrected Regulations which he had then received, and that he did not recollect exhibiting them to the committee, but thought he had, and believed that when he reported the amendments to the House, he had the corrected copy and deposited it with the Clerk with the intent that from that copy the system should be published. These recollections were not, however, sustained by the other members of the committee nor by the Clerk of the House. None of them apparently had ever seen the corrected copy *before* the passage of the law, but the Clerk of the House thought he had seen it *subsequently*, when General Smyth made a return to him of various papers which had been before the committee, and he refused to receive it, not considering himself the proper repository. Search had been made in his office, but it could not be found.

The select committee reported that it was an act of omission, and not of design, on the part of the chairman of the Military Committee in not submitting the corrected copy to the committee.

The committee reported, May 6, 1822,[1] and Congress immediately passed an act—which was approved May 7—repealing the fourteenth section of the act of 1821.

General Gaines was accused by General Scott with being instrumental in raising the opposition to these regulations.

4. By an act of Congress of July 28, 1866, the Secretary of War was directed to have prepared, and to report to Congress, at its next session, a code of regulations for the government of the Army and of the militia in actual service, including rules for the government of courts-martial, the existing regulations (those of 1863) to remain in force until Congress should have acted on such report—not, as it has been erroneously stated, until Congress should otherwise provide.

It was said by the Court of Claims (13 Ct. Cls., 6), and repeated by Attorney General Brewster, that

---

[1] For the report of this committee (containing General Scott's explanation), see American State Papers, Vol. XIII, p. 422. General Scott's explanation is given in Appendix E. See also Winthrop's **Military Law and Precedents**, p. 23.

under the act of 1866 a report of a code of regulations for the government of the Army was made but not acted on. This was evidently a mistake; a system of regulations was prepared by a board consisting of Generals Sherman, Sheridan, and Augur, but it does not appear to have been submitted to Congress. A revision of the Articles of War was reported, but not, it would seem, a code of regulations.

The act of 1866 was construed by the Court of Claims, the Attorney General, the Second Comptroller, and Secretary of War Belknap[1] to have had the effect of an adoption by Congress of the regulations of 1863, but there has been little agreement as to how long the regulations so adopted remained in force. The legislation has sometimes been regarded as repealed by the repeal provisions (section 5596) of the Revised Statutes, if not already superseded by the act of July 15, 1870, which again provided for the preparation of a system of regulations, to be reported to Congress "at its next session." It has also been held that the regulations of 1863 remained in force, by

---

[1] In submitting to Congress, February 17, 1873, a system of regulations prepared in accordance with the provisions of an act of July 15, 1870, Secretary Belknap said: "The regulations then and now in force are those of 1863. They are ten years old, and no longer adapted to the condition of Army affairs, but under the act of 1866 it is impossible for the Executive to change them. The length of a letter on a knapsack, for example, being prescribed therein, the Executive has no power to alter its size until Congress shall authorize it, and the regulations now presented will be subject to precisely the same objection, and if they are to be made law, not to be altered or amended save by act of Congress, there are many provisions that it would be wise not to present, as experience may show that alterations may be necessary. The Secretary of War, therefore, earnestly recommends to Congress that, if formally approved by that body, they be made subject *to such alterations as the President may from time to time adopt.*"

virtue of the legislation of 1866, until superseded by the regulations of 1881, issued under the act of July 23, 1879, authorizing the Secretary of War to cause all the regulations of the Army and general orders then in force to be codified and published.[1] And they have been treated as in force subsequently to this. According to Second Comptroller Maynard, in 1886 (Dig. Opin. Second Comptroller, VIII, sec. 867), and the Court of Claims, in 1888 (23 Ct. Cls., 461), they were in force at those dates, by virtue of the legislation of 1866.

Two codes of regulations have been issued since then, but not under any act of Congress.[2] If, therefore, the regulations of 1863 were in fact in force, by legislative adoption, at the time of the issue of the last two codes (1889 and 1895), as they were if the Second Comptroller and the Court of Claims were correct, they were not legally alterable by the later codes, and are not legally alterable by executive action now, and all the actual alterations of rules that have been thus in fact made are invalid, and the regulations of 1863 are still legally in force. But they were not.

The legislation of 1866 was undoubtedly repealed by section 5596 of the Revised Statutes, if it was in force up to the date of their enactment. That it was repealed by the legislation of 1870 does not appear to be true, because the provisions of the latter never took effect. But it would seem to have expired by virtue of its own terms at the end of the second session of the Thirty-ninth Congress, when the report

---

[1] Attorney General Brewster, 17 Opin., 463.
[2] The legislation of 1875, hereafter described, considered by the light of its history, is believed to have been carried out, and satisfied by the promulgation of the regulations of 1881.

called for not having been made, and it being no longer possible to make it at that session, as required, the legislation became inoperative. The regulations of 1863 existed from that time on (and, if not, certainly after the enactment of the Revised Statutes) as an ordinary executive code, not stamped with legislative adoption, but liable to be superseded, and in fact superseded, by the first code issued thereafter.

CHAPTER IV.

THE DIFFERENT EDITIONS OF ARMY REGULATIONS.

The following information with reference to the different editions of Army Regulations, although but a brief sketch of the history of their adoption, will, it is believed, present the matter in a form convenient for future use.

Prior to the adoption of the Constitution, Congress (which then constituted the Government) provided, from time to time, for regulations for the Army, principally for the government of the staff corps. In some cases the Board of War, then consisting of civilians, was directed to make regulations. (2 Journals of Congress, 432, 520; 3 *id.*, 328.) In others, chiefs of the different corps were so authorized; as the Quartermaster General, for certain classes of his employees (*id.*, 126; 3 *id.*, 253, 496); the Inspector General (3 *id.*, 203, 523, 525); the Director of Military Hospitals (*id.*, 527); and the Medical Board (*id.*, 705). The Secretary of War, after one was appointed by Congress, was, in addition to his general duties, required to "regulate," or "direct," as to certain special subjects—as the making of payments and returns and keeping of accounts by regimental paymasters (4 Journals, 7), the making and transmitting of returns by officers generally (*id.*,

9), and the duties of the commissary general of prisoners (*id.*).¹

In 1779 (March 29) the Continental Congress adopted certain "Regulations," to "be observed by all the troops of the United States." These had been prepared by Baron Steuben, and were published in the same year as "Regulations for the order and discipline of the troops of the United States." They were, for the greater part, a system of tactics and rules for the camp and on the march, but contained "Instructions" for the different regimental officers and enlisted men. Another edition of these "Regulations" was published in 1809, by M. Carey, of Philadelphia.

On the increase of the Army in 1798, in contemplation of war with a foreign power, President Adams issued manuscript regulations, supplemental to Baron Steuben's, containing many rules prescribing duties of the different grades of officers and enlisted men in service, and particularly as to the administration in a garrisoned post or barracks.

In 1808 a little volume containing the Articles of War and certain regulations with reference to allowances and promotion was published in Washington—apparently by authority—by "Dinsmore and Cooper."

Many of the regulations in force at the beginning of the year 1810, and which had been issued at different times since 1797, in the form of General and Executive Orders, are given in Duane's Military Dictionary.²

---

¹ Winthrop's Military Law, p. 21, note 3. And see, generally, the subject of "Regulations for the Army," as discussed by this author.

² In this work (published in Philadelphia in 1810) it was said: "There is no coherent or consistent system of regulations in existence for the military establishment of the United States.

In 1812 the statutes relating to the military establishment and the existing regulations relating to allowances, promotion, and the duties of the staff were collected together and published in book form. These regulations are also to be found in the appendix to Maltby on Courts-Martial.

The regulations of 1813 have already been mentioned. They may be regarded as the first of our series of codes of Army Regulations, the preceding publications, of 1808 and 1812, making no pretense to the establishment of a complete system, but merely

---

The economy of military arrangement is as essential as the discipline of the field, to assure the effects of military operations. There should be a well digested system of regulations, and upon that system should be engrafted a staff, susceptible of adaptation to the peace or the war establishment, to the smallest or the largest force. The French have derived the greatest advantage from their regulations, which have been formed by a well digested body of principles adapted to all circumstances, and the enforcement and execution of which is always distinctly appropriated to the proper officers of the staff. At present the regulations of the United States Army is confined to a few general orders from the War Department, on detached points of service; and of occasional orders of the commander-in-chief, issued upon some exigency, at remote periods, and adopted into permanent use. In many instances these regulations have been altered by the War Office, in others the circumstances which gave rise to them have ceased, and the regulations become obsolete or inappropriate. In 1810, an attempt was made, by the establishment of a Quartermaster General's Office, to commence something like a system; should this be accomplished it may be beneficial, though the want of information in the duties of a staff, particularly if those heretofore arranged under the Quartermaster General's Department alone are to be adopted, that it is to be feared the system may remain defective, should the old English model, now exploded by the British themselves, be kept in view instead of the more enlarged system introduced in modern wars. The treatise on the staff by *Grimoard*, contains the best body of regulations extant. It has been translated and will form a part of the American Military Library.

"The following are among the principal regulations in force at the beginning of the year 1810:"

[Then follow the regulations referred to.]

republishing a few existing regulations. The greater part of this publication is, however, also taken up with a republication of statutes. The part of it devoted to regulations would not equal 20 pages of our present Regulations.

Editions of Army Regulations were also issued in 1814, 1816, 1817, and 1820. Those of 1817 and 1820 were republications of the edition of 1816, with the addition of regulations issued by the War Department subsequently. These Regulations may be found in the Library of Congress. Another edition was published in 1815, by Webster & Skinners, of Albany, New York, but this was not an authorized edition.

An edition was also issued in 1821, under the circumstances already described.

The next edition was that of 1825. It was a revision by General Scott of his Regulations of 1821.[1]

In 1834 a system of general regulations for the Army was published by Francis P. Blair, of Washington. A copy of it is in the War Department Library. It was not an authorized edition, but seems substantially to coincide with that which was published in 1835 by authority and is known as the

---

[1] A number of important regulations were published in 1833, in Order, No. 48, of that year—"The 48th Commandment," as it seems to have been called. (Military and Naval Magazine, September, 1834.) In an article copied into this magazine from the "American Quarterly Review," in 1833, it was said: "Under the presidentship of Mr. Monroe, and the secretaryship of Mr. Calhoun, a new era was formed in our national defence, the beneficial influences of which will continue to be felt as long as we are a free nation. Our present system of accountableness and responsibility was then established. * * * From that period the War Department has held a new rank in the Cabinet, and assumed a corresponding elevation in popular opinion. Previously, it had been regarded merely as the headquarters of the Army."

Macomb Regulations, having been revised by General Macomb. Some amendments to these were made in an order from the War Department, dated December 31, 1836, in which it was declared that the General Order prefixed to the Regulations of 1835 had never been promulgated, nor been in force, and directing the page containing it to be canceled, and the order of December 31, 1836, to be inserted in its place.

Another edition of Army Regulations was issued in 1841, and a revision by Gen. E. D. Townsend in 1847.

The next edition was that of 1857, when Jefferson Davis was Secretary of War, and sometimes, on this account, called the "Jeff. Davis Regulations." Tradition seems to connect Gen. Don Carlos Buell with the preparation of these Regulations, but there is no record of it.

The Regulations of 1847 contained the following article:

ARTICLE X.

THE COMMANDER OF THE ARMY.

48. The military establishment is placed under the orders of the Major-General Commanding-in-Chief, in all that regards its discipline and military control. Its fiscal arrangements properly belong to the administrative departments of the staff, and to the Treasury Department under the direction of the Secretary of War.

49. The General will watch over the economy of the service, in all that relates to the expenditure of money, supply of arms, ordnance, and ordnance-stores, clothing, equipments, camp-equipage, medical and hospital stores, barracks, quarters, transportation, fortifications, Military Academy, pay and subsistence—in short, everything which enters into the expenses of the military establishment, whether personal

or national. He will also see that the estimates for the military service are based upon proper data, and made for the objects contemplated by law, and necessary to the due support and useful employment of the Army. In carrying into effect these important duties, he will call to his counsel and assistance the staff, and those officers proper in his opinion to be employed in verifying and inspecting all the objects which may require attention. The rules and regulations established for the government of the Army, and the laws relating to the military establishment, are the guides to the Commanding General in the performance of his duties.

This article (and General Scott laid stress on the fact that it was drawn up with care under the eye of Secretary Marcy, and approved by President Polk during his absence in Mexico) was omitted from the Regulations of 1857, and a bitter attack on the Secretary of War by General Scott followed. An account of the controversy which thus arose, as well as of the circumstances that led up to it, is given in a paper by Mr. W. A. DeCaindry, on "The establishment of the War Department as one of the Executive Departments of the United States Government, with a general view of its interior organization and administration," published in 1878, as an appendix to the report of the Joint Committee of Congress on the Regulations of the Army. General Fry, in his work on brevets, gives a copy of General Scott's objections to the Regulations of 1857, and of Secretary Floyd's reply, in which latter occurs the following passage:

"The failure to insert in the new regulations a definition of the duties and authority pertaining to the office of Commander in Chief of the Army, which was contained in the old regulations, I am satisfied, does not, in any degree, take from it any power, authority, honor or command conferred upon that high office by law. Definitions are always difficult, sometimes impossible. The definitions in the old regulations, attempting to define the duties of the principal officers of the Army, are not, in my judgment, satisfactory; and I think the new regulations wisely follow the example set by those which you prepared in 1825, in which no definitions were attempted."

The regulations in question were never restored.

The Regulations of 1861 were a repetition of those of 1857, with, however, some modifications. There is a remarkable lack of information in the War Department in regard to the preparation of this code.

The Regulations of 1863 were prepared by General Breck, and were issued under the authority of Secretary of War Stanton. They contain the previous Army Regulations of 1861, except an entirely new regulation for the Subsistence Department, which was approved separately; and they omit those for the Engineer Department, and are supplemented by an appendix containing "changes and additions to the Army Regulations up to June 25, 1863." As this was not a complete revision of the regulations, Mr. Stanton preferred to leave the original order (of the Regulations of 1861) for its observance in the new edition, and to publish it as the Regulations of 1861, with the additions above described.

The legislation of 1866, as affecting the Regulations of 1863, has already been discussed. This legislation required the Secretary of War to have prepared and to report to Congress at its next session a code of regulations for the government of the Army. The draft of a code was prepared by General Townsend, and was submitted to a board convened in December, 1867, consisting of Generals Sherman, Sheridan, and Augur. In February, 1868, the board reported the completion of their duties, and submitted the regulations, revised by them, and approved by General Grant. June 12. 1868, General Schofield, Secretary of War, made a communication to Congress, in which he said:

"A very carefully prepared system of Regulations for the Army and Militia is now in my hands awaiting the action which may be taken on the Rules and Articles of War, with a view to making any alterations in them which may be required if the said Rules and Articles should be changed.

"In my judgment, however, it would be unwise to subject a code of General Regulations for the Army to the formal action of Congress, thus giving them a fixed character, unalterable except by the same formal action. All matter in the Regulations which should properly be bound by force of law is actually made in exact conformity with military acts of Congress, and is always, when practicable, in the precise language of the laws. But there are very many matters of detail which depend upon the daily changing necessities of the service, and are regulated by the experience and intelligence of practical men in the Army, which should be left for modification, as often as circumstances demand, to the discretion of the Secretary of War and the President. It is a principle, well understood and invariably acted upon, that whenever a regulation becomes in conflict with a law of Congress, it is null and void. The law is thus, as it were, a constitution, and regulations are simply the by-laws based thereon.

"The authority to make alterations in the Regulations was vested by act of April 24, 1816, in the Secretary of War, with the approval of the President, and has been ever since so exercised with this exception, that by an act of March 2, 1821, a system prepared by General Scott, under an act of March 3, 1813, "was approved and adopted." But this act of March 2, 1821, was repealed, in terms, by an act of May 7, 1822, leaving the act of April 24, 1816, still in operation. The Army Regulations are always public and easy of reference, and Congress can readily at any time correct, by legislation, an objectionable feature which may appear in them.

"I recommend that so much of section 37, act of July 28, 1866, as requires this code of Regulations to be reported to Congress, be repealed. Its several parts have been prepared by officers of the largest experience and greatest familiarity with the operations of their particular branches of the Army, and the whole system has been very carefully examined, arranged, and harmonized by a board of the first officers in the Army. It has received the approval of General Grant, who has been consulted on all important points."

No further action was taken with reference to the system of Regulations prepared by the Sherman Board. In submitting it to the Secretary of War, the board remarked:

"It has been our earnest endeavor to make this system as simple, plain, and consistent in all its parts as possible, and to make no changes from established usages, except where we were convinced by actual experience that they were necessary to the service. The regulations for the staff departments are all based substantially on the recommendations of the present heads of departments, save and except that we place all the heads of departments in the same relation to the General of the Army as the law already places him, the General, in relation to the President, the constitutional Commander-in-Chief. We have also endeavored more clearly to define the relative duties of the Secretary of War and the General-in-Chief. Their relative spheres of duty are so important, and harmony of action on their part is so directly reflected by the Army itself, that we think too much importance can not be given to this branch of the subject."

The following were the regulations with reference to the duties of the General-in-Chief proposed by this board:

"1. The military establishment is under the orders of the General of the Army in all that regards its discipline and military control. Its fiscal arrangements properly belong to the administrative departments of the staff, and to the Treasury Department, under the direction of the Secretary of War.

"2. The headquarters of the General of the Army shall be at the city of Washington, and all orders and instructions relating to military operations issued by the President or Secretary of War shall be issued through the General of the Army, and, in case of his inability, through the next in rank. The General of the Army shall not be removed, suspended, or relieved from command, or assigned to duty elsewhere than at said headquarters, except at his own request, without the previous approval of the Senate; and any orders or instructions relating to military operations issued contrary to these requirements shall be null and void;

and any officer who shall issue orders or instructions contrary to the provisions of this law shall be deemed guilty of a misdemeanor in office; and any officer of the Army who shall transmit, convey, or obey any orders or instructions so issued contrary to the provisions of this section, knowing that such orders were so issued, shall be liable to imprisonment for not less than two nor more than twenty years, upon conviction thereof in any court of competent jurisdiction.

"3. The General will watch over the economy of the service, in all that relates to the expenditure of money, supply of arms, ordnance, and ordnance-stores, clothing, equipments, camp-equipage, medical and hospital stores, barracks, quarters, transportation, fortifications, Military Academy, pay and subsistence—in short, everything which enters into the expenses of the military establishment. He will see that the estimates for the military service are based upon proper data, and made for the objects contemplated by law, and necessary to the due support and useful employment of the Army. He will call to his counsel and assistance the staff, and those officers proper in his opinion to be employed in verifying and inspecting all the objects which may require attention. The rules and regulations established for the government of the Army, and the laws relating to the military establishment, are the guides to the General in the performance of his duties."

The regulation numbered 2 was copied from a provision of the Army Appropriation Act of March 2, 1867, which, as the President declared in a message to Congress, deprived him of his constitutional functions as commander-in-chief, but which he was compelled to countenance, as by withholding his signature he would defeat necessary appropriations. The legislation, enacted for a clearly unconstitutional purpose, was repealed in the Army Appropriation Act of July 15, 1870, when the political conditions were changed. It was not, indeed, quietly submitted to by the President, who on the 3d of September, 1867, issued his proclamation in which officers of the Army and Navy were reminded that in accepting their commissions they incurred the obligation to observe, obey, and follow such directions as they might from time to time receive from the President, or the General, or other superior officers set over them, according to the rules and discipline of war, and were enjoined, in this direct manner, to assist and sustain the courts and other civil authorities of the United States in the administration of the laws.

By an act of July 15, 1870 (16 Stat., 319), Congress prescribed:

"That the Secretary of War shall prepare a system of general regulations for the administration of the affairs of the Army, which, when approved by Congress, shall be in force and obeyed until altered or revoked by the same authority; and said regulations shall be reported to Congress at its next session: *Provided*, That said regulations shall not be inconsistent with the laws of the United States."

Pursuant to this legislation, the Marcy Board was convened July 3, 1871. The members of this Board were Col. R. B. Marcy, J. H. King, and H. J. Hunt, and Majors R. I. Dodge and A. J. Alexander. During November and December, 1871, and January, 1872, the report of the Board was critically considered by the

Secretary of War, by whom Asst. Adjt. Gen. Thomas M. Vincent, as the representative of the Secretary, had been associated with the Board for the purpose of a further consideration of the proposed system. The system of regulations thus finally prepared by this Board was submitted to Congress by Secretary of War Belknap, February 17th, 1873 (see Appendix F), and was published as H. R. Report No. 85, Forty-second Congress, third session. On the 13th of May, 1874, the Military Committee of the House made a report on the subject (Appendix G), concluding with a recommendation of the legislation subsequently (March 1, 1875) enacted. It provided:

"That so much of section twenty of the act approved July fifteenth, eighteen hundred and seventy, entitled 'An act making appropriations for the support of the Army for the year ending June thirtieth, eighteen hundred and seventy-one, and for other purposes,' as requires the system of general regulations for the Army therein authorized to be reported to Congress at its next session, and approved by that body, be, and the same is hereby, repealed; and the President is hereby authorized, under said section, to make and publish regulations for the government of the Army in accordance with existing laws."

In 1876, a compilation was prepared by Capt. R. N. Scott, and printed under the following authentication:

"WAR DEPARTMENT, *July 1, 1876.*

"These regulations are a compilation of all rules for the government of the Army, which were in force January 1, 1876, and are based upon the Army Regulations of 1863, as altered or amended by orders, circulars, decisions, and laws passed since the latter year. Compiled, under the direction of the Secretary of War, by Capt. R. N. Scott, U. S. Army.

"H. T. CROSBY.
"*Chief Clerk.*"

This compilation was printed, but was not published to the Army, and, notwithstanding the foregoing indorsement, was not an authorized code. The records of the War Department seem to furnish no further information with regard to the circumstances of its preparation, but it may have been the final arrangement of a compilation made by Mr. John Tweedale, which consisted of the Regulations of 1863, brought to date, agreeably to subsequent orders and amendments.

Just a month before this General Sherman had called attention to the necessity of a revision of the Army Regulations, and had recommended that the work of preparing a new code be assigned to General Schofield. Fortunately, he said, the task would be rendered comparatively light by the fact that two systems of regulations had already been prepared and were in print; one compiled in 1868–69 by a board consisting of Generals Sherman, Sheridan, and Augur, and the other compiled by the "Marcy Board" in 1873. It would, he thought, be preferable to have a single officer assigned to this work, rather than a board, because a board would be apt to begin *de novo* and go again over the very ground already well studied by previous boards.

General Schofield entered upon this work, agreeably to General Sherman's recommendations, but no system of regulations prepared by him was published. The first five articles of such a system were, however, printed, and referred to heads of staff departments for remark. One of the articles was as follows:

"The chiefs of the several staff corps, departments, and bureaus of the Army sustain the twofold relation of chiefs of bureaus of the War Department and chiefs of staff to the General of the Army. They act under the immediate direction and control of the Secretary of War, in respect to all matters of accountability and administration not immediately connected with military operations; they report directly to and act under the immediate orders of the General in Chief in all matters appertaining to the command of the Army; they are the repositories of the laws and regulations for the government of the military service and of the knowledge which experience in their respective departments affords; they are the advisers and agents alike of the Secretary of War and of the General in Chief, and upon the proper exercise of their functions, in this twofold relation, depends the harmonious working of the complex system of military administration and command."

This was opposed by most of the heads of the staff departments, and was defended by General Schofield. A part of the discussion, including General Schofield's remarks, was published in the above-mentioned report of the Joint Committee on the Reorganization of the Army (of which General Burnside was chairman), as were also the proposed articles which contained the disputed propositions. In the elaborate bill which

[1] For General Schofield's recollection of this matter, see Appendix H.

was reported by the committee, and which was intended, together with certain unchanged chapters of the Revised Statutes, to be a "condensed and complete military code," the general officers' view was adopted. On a later occasion the relation of the staff departments to the General in Chief was again the subject of consideration, and on this occasion the Secretary of War (Mr. Lincoln) gave his views at some length on the other side of the question, and decided it accordingly.[5]

For another discussion of the subject of the command of the Army, see an article by General Schofield in the Century Magazine for August, 1897. See also, "The Command of the Army," in Fry's Miscellanies.

In Scott's Military Dictionary, published in 1864, we find the following statement: "Administration and command are distinct. Administration is controlled by the head of an executive department of the government, under the orders of the President, by means of legally appointed administrative agents, with or without rank, while command, or the discipline, military control, and direction of military service of officers and soldiers, can be legally exercised only by the military hierarchy, at the head of which is the constitutional Commander in Chief of the Army, Navy, and militia, followed by the commander of the Army, and other military grades created by Congress." (Title "Administration;" and see also titles "Regulations" and "Army Regulations.") Colonel Scott did not recognize the constitutional power of the President to make Army regulations.

In England the powers of the "commander in chief" [i. e., the commanding general of the army] were at first much more extensive than they are now; in fact the King deputed to him all his own military powers in their full effect, and the commander in chief exercised the functions which are now divided between the secretary at war and the commander in chief. He could frame articles of war; he could order out militia; he granted all commissions, as well of administrative officers as of others; he issued warrants for payments; and he prepared the estimates for the establishment. When a secretary-at-war was appointed he was made subordinate to the commander in chief; in fact the latter was independent of all control but that of the sovereign, and was the sole head and chief of all military organization, administrative as well as disciplinary. (Walton's History of the British Standing Army, 1660 to 1700.)

About this time, namely, August 15, 1876, Congress passed a joint resolution to the following effect:

"Whereas the President was, by an act of Congress, approved March first, eighteen hundred and seventy-five, authorized to make and publish regulations for the government of the Army, in accordance with existing laws; and

"Whereas by an act of Congress, approved July twenty-four, eighteen hundred and seventy-six, a commission was created to which has been referred the whole subject-matter of reform and reorganization of the Army of the United States; therefore

"*Resolved by the Senate and House of Representatives of the United States of America in Congress assembled,* That the President be requested to postpone all action in connection with the publication of said regulations until after the report of said commission is received and acted on by Congress at its next session."

On the 7th of March, 1878, a bill was introduced in the Senate to provide for a code of Army Regulations. The bill having been referred to the Secretary of War for such suggestions as he might deem proper, Secretary of War McCrary said that he adhered to the opinion that the President should be authorized to make and publish regulations for the government of the Army, but if it be required that such regulations should be submitted to Congress, to be by that body approved before being issued, he recommended early action. A copy of Secretary McCrary's remarks on the same subject, in his annual report for 1877, will be found in Appendix I.

On the 15th of August, 1878, the clerk of the Committee on Military Affairs of the Senate transmitted to the Secretary of War a copy of a Senate resolution of June 18th, authorizing a subcommittee, for the purpose of considering the revision of the Army Regulations, and stated that he had been directed to cooperate with the War Department in every possible way and to report to the committee the revision of the regulations made under the direction of the Secretary of War. But by act of June 23, 1879 (21 Stats., 34), Congress disposed of the whole matter by authorizing and directing the Secretary of War to cause all the regulations of the Army and general orders then in force to be codified and published to the Army.

The Regulations of 1881 were the outcome of this legislation. In July, 1880, a board was convened for the purpose of examining and reporting upon the codification of the regulations made pursuant to its requirements. It consisted of Generals McDowell and Meigs, Colonels Sackett, Hazen, and Upton, with Maj. A. H. Nickerson as recorder. General McDowell was, however, almost immediately relieved and General Auger substituted in his stead. The board received the following instructions, communicated to them by the Adjutant General:

"In submitting the accompanying codification of the laws, regulations, and orders made in pursuance of the requirements of section 2 of an act approved June 23, 1879, the Secretary of War instructs me to say that he desires the board of officers to examine the codification to ascertain whether its parts are consistently arranged; whether there are inaccuracies resulting from misinterpretation; whether there are any repetitions or instances where the phraseology may not clearly express the exact meaning, and that there are no contradictions. Wherever these defects are discovered it will be the duty of the board to propose a substitute for the defective paragraph and submit it in its report for the Secretary's action.

"It is no part of the functions of the board to *make* regulations, but simply by a careful examination to detect errors and report what changes may be considered requisite for a proper fulfillment of the law under which the codification was made.

"It is the Secretary's desire that when these regulations are published to the Army they shall form as perfect a code as possible and be so free from errors as not to require correction or immediate modification."

On the 13th of September the board was dissolved.

In a note at the beginning of the Regulations of 1881 it is stated that "the work of codification was confided to the Adjutant General of the Army," and, in fact, the codification submitted to the board by the Adjutant General (Drum) was prepared by Adjutant General Townsend. A characteristic of these regulations, and one which makes them still valuable, is that they give the source and authority of the individual regulations. An "Abridged Edition" of them was also issued.

After this no revision of the Regulations appears to have been undertaken until December, 1886, when a board was appointed, consisting of General Benét, Colonel (now General) Otis, Lieut. Col. R. N. Scott, and Lieut. (now Lieut. Col.) George B. Davis, "for the purpose of revising and condensing the Regulations of the Army and preparing a new edition of the same." Colonel Scott died two months later. The work of this board finally took the form of the Regulations of 1889.

There remains to be considered only the Regulations of 1895. General Kelton, in December, 1891, called attention to the necessity of a revision, and in February, 1892, General Schofield wrote as follows:

"The need has become urgent of a new edition of the Revised Regulations. The need is not so much for any revision of the existing regulations as for a new publication of the regulations as they now exist; that is to say, the Regulations of 1889 as revised since their publication. That edition having been very hastily published, and hence very imperfect, it has been amended in so many details and in some cases frequently, that a new publication of the regulations as they exist to-day is of vital importance.

"The revision that has been going on during the last three years, or nearly three years, has involved very great labor and very careful consideration of the several subjects on the part of many officers, including the chiefs of bureaus, the Commanding General, and the Secretary of War. So much of the regulations as have been so revised ought, in my judgment, not to be changed without cogent reasons.

"The revision of regulations is a very delicate work, and in past experience has generally resulted in an exceedingly imperfect code, requiring numerous amendments. Regulations are a matter of gradual growth, and should be preserved as a rule in the form which has resulted from such growth. In some cases, doubtless, obsolete regulations may be eliminated and others may be somewhat simplified, and some which were carelessly omitted in the last revision should be restored. The officer charged with the revision should be instructed to consider very carefully all such questions, consult the chiefs of bureaus of the War Department, and after obtaining concurrent views upon each question, submit it for the consideration of the Commanding General, and finally for the approval of the Secretary of War, before incorporating it in the revised edition.

"In this way, as suggested by the Adjutant General, a satisfactory work may be accomplished, ready for publication as soon as it is completed and duly indexed."

This revision passed through the hands of Col. (now Adjutant General) H. C. Corbin, Maj. (now Lieut. Col.) J. C. Gilmore, and Maj. (now Lieut. Col.) J. B. Babcock, constituting a board, and afterwards through the hands of the Adjutant General and the Major General Commanding the Army. Gen. E. S. Otis also went over the work. But the preparation of this revision was finally in charge of the Assistant Secretary of War, Maj. (now Lieut. Col.) George W. Davis, and Capt. J. T. French. One of its distinguishing features is that the regulations which relate more particularly to the management of the business of the staff departments, and do not affect the Army at large, are omitted from the general regulations and embodied in separate manuals. Necessarily, however, these manuals cover a wider field than this would indicate. The general Regulations, with their accompaniment of manuals, may be regarded as forming the Regulations of 1895. One of these manuals—the Manual for Courts-Martial—is not, indeed, a staff manual at all, but is a general system of rules for the administration of military justice. It is the first of its kind promulgated by the War Department, and is an outgrowth and enlargement of the directions on the subject which it was formerly the practice to issue from the headquarters of military departments. Regulations, approved by the Secretary of War, had, however, before this been issued by several of the staff departments for their own government.

The regulations for the United States Military Academy also emanate from the President's constitutional power.

There can be no doubt, however, that, within limits, the Superintendent of the United States Military Academy, the same as any officer in control of a public institution peopled with persons whose good conduct is intrusted to his charge, may also lay down rules or regulations. He does in fact exercise this power in issuing certain orders. A distinction has, indeed, been made between regulations and orders, but it can not be said that there is any essential difference between regulations and general orders laying down general rules of action.

As a good illustration of this power, as vested in superintendents of institutions of this character, we may take the various Soldiers' Homes. For these certain regulations are prescribed by statute and others by their boards of managers, necessarily, however, leaving a very considerable residue of matters, principally relating to discipline, to be regulated by the governors of the institutions. It may, of course, sometimes be difficult to decide what the limit of the power is, but that the power exists seems clear. Without it public institutions of this kind could not be controlled, and therefore could not be managed for the purposes for which they are established.

Commanding officers of military posts have this power in a marked degree—limited, it is true, in their case also, by statute and regulation of higher authority, but, subject to these, having a distinct, necessary, and unquestioned jurisdiction. In this case, however, as also in the case of the Superintendent of the Military Academy, the power is a part of an independent system, namely, the military system. But it is the same kind of power. And it is the same kind of power that is exercised by the school teacher in the maintenance of the discipline of his school.

"When no rules and regulations have been prescribed by the

board, the teacher is authorized to make such reasonable rules as shall best promote the welfare of his school and secure order and discipline therein. And even where rules have been prescribed by the board, the teacher may, unless expressly prohibited, make such additional rules and requirements as special cases or sudden emergencies may render necessary." (Meachem on Public Officers, 728.) And see American and English Encyclopedia of Law, title, "Master and Servant," vol. 14, p. 858.

Ship captains possess this authority in a peculiar degree. Justice Story, discussing the relation of the officers of a ship to the seamen, said:

"The learned counsel for the defendant has asked the court to direct the jury, that the officers of the ship are clothed, not merely with a civil, but with a military power, over the seamen on board. In my judgment, that is not the true relation of the parties. The authority to compel obedience, and to inflict punishment, is, indeed, of a summary character, but, in no just sense, of a military character. It is entirely civil; and far more resembles the authority of a parent over his children, or rather, that of a master over his servant or apprentice, than that of a commander over his soldiers. Properly speaking, however, the authority of the officers over the seamen of a ship, is of a peculiar character, and drawn from the usages, and customs, and necessities of the maritime naval service, and founded upon principles applicable to that relation, which is full of difficulties and perils, and requires extraordinary restraints, and extraordinary discipline, and extraordinary promptitude and obedience to orders." (United States v. Hunt, 26 Fed. Cases, 135.)

Commanders of naval vessels possess the power also, and being officers in command of public armed ships they have even greater discretion. (Wilkes v. Dinsman, 7 How., 89.)

In a greater or less degree, according to the conditions, the power to make rules of action or regulations must exist wherever there are rulers and ruled. In military commands the strictest discipline is necessary, and for the purpose of maintaining this discipline a military jurisdiction, or military law, exists, which is quite independent and free from interference within its own special scope. But in a general sense it is certainly true that wherever the relation of ruler and ruled is legally established there must be a power of control, in which, subject to such limitations as may legally be imposed, is included the power to make regulations.

CHAPTER V.

THE INTERPRETATION AND CONSTRUCTION OF REGULATIONS.

"Interpretation is the art of finding out the true sense of any form of words; that is, the sense which their author intended to convey, and of enabling others to derive from them the same idea which the author intended to convey." "Construction is the drawing of conclusions respecting subjects that lie beyond the direct expression of the text, from elements known from and given in the text—conclusions which are in the spirit, though not within the letter, of the text."[1]

---

[1] Legal and Political Hermenentics, by Francis Lieber, pp. 11, 44.

"Interpretation differs from construction in that the former is the art of finding out the true sense of any form of words; that is, the sense which their author intended to convey; and of enabling others to derive from them the same idea which the author intended to convey. Construction, on the other hand, is the drawing of conclusions, respecting subjects that lie beyond the direct expressions of the text, from elements known from and given in the text; conclusions which are in the spirit, though not within the letter of the text. Interpretation only takes place if the text conveys some meaning or other. But construction is resorted to when, in comparing two different writings of the same individual, or two different enactments by the same legislative body, there is found contradiction where there was evidently no intention of such contradiction one of another, or where it happens that part of a writing or declaration contradicts the rest. When this is the case, and the nature of the document or declaration, or whatever else it may be, is such as not to allow us to consider the whole as being invalidated by a partial or other contradiction, then resort must be had to construction; so, too, if required to act in cases which have not been foreseen by the framers of those rules, by which we are nevertheless obliged, for some binding reason, faithfully to regulate as well as we can our action respecting the unforeseen case." (Cooley, Constitutional Limitations, 51.)

"There can be no sound interpretation without good faith and common sense. The object of all interpretation and construction is to ascertain the intention of the authors, even so far as to control the literal signification of the words; for *verba ita sunt intelligenda ut res magis valeat quam pereat.* Words are, therefore, to be taken as those who used them intended, which must be presumed to be in their popular and ordinary signification, unless there is some good reason for supposing otherwise, as where technical terms are used; *quoties in verba nulla est ambiguitas, ibi nulla expositio contra verba fienda est.*"[1]

The underlying principles of true interpretation and construction apply to all language, in whatever form it may be used, although there are principles applicable only to its special uses, as in constitutions, statutes, executive regulations, or contracts. The rules for the interpretation and construction of executive regulations closely resemble those for the interpretation and construction of statutes.[2]

1. The first practical question which suggests itself is: Does each new edition of the Army Regulations entirely displace the preceding one, both as to the subjects treated of and those omitted?

It is a principle of statutory construction that when the legislature makes a revision of a statute, and frames a new statute upon the subject-matter, and from the framework of the act it is apparent that the legislature designed a complete scheme for the matter, it is a legislative declaration that whatever is embraced in

---

[1] Francis Lieber: subject, "Interpretation." Bouvier's Law Dictionary.
[2] Devereux, 148.

the new law shall prevail, and whatever is excluded is discarded.¹ And this principle is applied to codifications. The general rule seems to be that statutes and parts of statutes omitted from a revision are to be considered as annulled, and are not to be revived by construction.² The practice with reference to the different editions of Army Regulations has conformed to this principle, each new edition being regarded as intended to be a substitute for the preceding one, and to displace it, both as to matter included in both editions, and matter included in the earlier but not in the later edition. It is the substitution of one compilation or system for another.³

2. What effect has such a new edition on existing orders relating to subjects covered by it, and on orders prescribing regulations not embodied in it?

The former, it would seem, are displaced by the new code, but the latter not; it being the understanding—subject to which the code is made—that it does not affect orders relating to subjects not embraced in it, nor in the preceding code. Such a question, for example, is understood to have once arisen with reference to General Orders No. 100, of 1863 (Instructions for the Government of the Armies of the United States in the Field), and to have been decided in favor of the permanency of these regulations.

The non-user of a statute does not repeal it, although it has been said that, on the principle that custom is of great force in the construction of statutes, long and

---

¹ Bracken v. Smith, 39 N. J. Eq., 169.
² Endlich. Interpretation of Statutes, sec. 202.
³ 17 Opin. Atty. Gen., 463.

uniform disuse might in some cases amount to a practical repeal. This would seem to apply even more strongly to regulations, which are made and executed by the same authority. The circumstances may be such that the long-continued disuse of a regulation would be significant of the understanding of the executive authority that it has become obsolete and inoperative.

3. The effect of the revocation of an army regulation by which a preceding regulation was revoked.

The principles regulating this differ somewhat from those of statutory construction. The latter have been thus stated:

"Where an act is repealed, and the repealing enactment is repealed by another, which manifests no intention that the first shall continue repealed, the common-law rule was (and in the absence of any statutory declaration to the contrary, the general rule still is), that the repeal of the second act revives the first; and revives it, too, *ab initio*, and not merely from the passing of the reviving act. (The revival of the original statute is also, in general, the effect of the expiration of a repealing statute by its own limitation, or of the suspension of the repealing act; and it is immaterial whether the repeal of the repealing act be express or by implication. Moreover, it extends, not only to statutes, but to the common law; so that, where an act superseding in any particular the common-law rule previously applicable is repealed, that rule is held to be revived. The doctrine stated is, however, not without exceptions, founded in the necessity of giving effect to the legislative intent. Thus, it is said that an absolute affirmative repeal of a statute by a subsequent one will survive the expiration of the latter by its own limitation; that the repeal of a statute which was a revision of, and which was intended as a substitute for, a former act to the same effect, will not revive the latter, such a result being manifestly contrary to the intent of the legislature; and that, for the same reason, the repeal of an act "amending another 'so as to read' in a given manner, which operates as a total merger of the amended act in the amending one, cannot revive the original statute.") (Endlich. Interpretation of Statutes, sec. 475.)

But with reference to Army regulations it would seem to be an established usage that the revocation of a regulation or an order, by which a preceding regulation or order was revoked, will not revive these, unless there be some express evidence of such an intention. This usage is no doubt founded on the necessity of certainty.

The revocation of a regulation which is simply declaratory of an established custom of the service would, however, in the absence of words indicating a different intention, doubtless be held to leave the custom in force. For example, a regulation of the Manual for Courts-Martial, which constitutes a part of the Army Regulations, says that the judge advocate of a court-martial swears the witnesses. This is declaratory of the custom of the service, for the ninety-second article of war, which prescribes the oath to be administered to witnesses, does not say by whom it shall be administered. Undoubtedly, the revocation of the regulation would leave the custom of the service in force.

4. *Expressio unius est exclusio alterius.* This rule applies in the construction of the Army Regulations, as well as in the construction of statutes. Where, for example, certain allowances are specified, other allowances for the same thing are excluded. Thus, it has been held by the War Department that the very fact that the Army Regulations do not provide for certain allowances claimed, raises a presumption that it was not the intention, when Army Regulations were published and promulgated by the direction of the Secretary of War, to make such allowances.[1]

But, apparently, even in the matter of allowances, a regulation, which has not been approved by Congress and is not made pursuant to an act of Congress, may be modified in a particular case, or the case may be taken out of its operation. Thus, it was held by the Assistant Comptroller of the Treasury (Mr. Bowers), with reference to the regulation prohibiting the reimbursement of Army officers who, when changing station, ship and pay for the transportation of their baggage, that "as the regulation was made by the Secretary of War, that officer has the power to amend it, or to waive its provisions in particular cases, but so long as the regulation stands as it does, no reimbursement can rightfully be made without the specific waiver of the regulation by the Secretary of War, when shipments are made by officers."[2] It is to be observed, however, that the Assistant Comptroller did not here make any distinction between regulations made pursuant to, or in execution of, a

---

[1] Claim of Captain Morton.
[2] 3 Dec. Comp. Treas., 305.

statute—in this case an appropriation act—and other regulations.

5. In construing Army regulations it is often necessary to consider to which of the classes named at the beginning of this work they belong; *i. e.*, those which have been approved and adopted by Congress; those made pursuant to, or in execution of, a statute; and those made by the President as commander-in-chief, but not falling under either of the other heads.

(*a*) Those which have been approved and adopted by Congress. These can not be modified or amended until the Congressional sanction has been removed. (See *ante*.)

(*b*) Those made pursuant to, or in execution of, a statute. These may be modified or amended, but individual exceptions to them can not be made. (See *ante*.)

(*c*) Those made by the President as commander-in-chief, and not falling under (*a*) or (*b*). These may be modified, and exceptions to them may be made. (See *ante*.)

We are ordinarily in the habit of regarding the different paragraphs of the Army Regulations as on the same footing in this respect, that is to say, as having the same degree of immutability; but this is, for the reason stated, believed to be a mistake likely to lead to faulty action. When we are considering the power of the President to modify, or make an exception to, a regulation, we ought to know to which of the above classes it belongs.

6. Authentic interpretation and construction.

"Authentic interpretation is called that which proceeds from the author or utterer of the text himself; properly speaking, therefore, it is no interpretation, but a declaration. If a legislative body, or monarch, give an interpretation, it is called authentic, though the same individuals who issued the law to be interpreted may not give the interpretation; because the successive assemblies or monarchs are considered as one and the same, making the law and giving the interpretation in their representative, and not in their personal characters. Authentic interpretation, therefore, need not always be correct, though it has, if formally given, binding power. Still it may be reversed by a subsequent law."[1]

In 1861 and 1862 the pay of officers of the Army was made up of pay proper and certain allowances, one of which was for a certain number of servants at the rate of pay, etc., of private soldiers. In 1861 the pay of private soldiers was increased, and in 1862 it was enacted that the legislation making this increase "shall not be so construed, after the passage of this act, as to increase the emoluments of the commissioned officers of the Army." This was an instance of authentic legislative construction. Executive construction of regulations is much more common, and is not limited to cases arising subsequently to the construction, but, on the contrary, is applied to existing cases. Because of this, and because there is in general no remedy in the nature of an appeal, it is incumbent on the authority construing the regulation to take great care to construe correctly.

7. Army regulations, like statutes, are not to be given a retroactive effect unless their language clearly requires it. (United States v. Webster, 28 Fed. Cases, 509; United States v. Davis, 132 U. S., 334; Dig. Opin.

---

[1] Lieber's Hermeneutics, p. 62.

Judge-Advocate General, 168.) We must, however, make an exception to this rule in favor of curative and declaratory regulations, the former being intended to cure matters of form, and the latter being explanatory of other regulations. But the presumption always is that the intention of the regulation is to lay down a rule for the future. If the intention is to give it a retroactive effect, it must clearly appear. This is applying to executive regulations a familiar rule of statutory construction.

"It is a proposition too well settled by authority to admit of dispute, or call for extended discussion, that curative acts, especially upon matters of public concern, are to be allowed the retroactive effect they are clearly intended to have, even though vested rights and decisions of courts be set aside by them, so long as they do not undertake to infuse life into proceedings utterly void for want of jurisdiction, and do not contravene the constitutional provisions against laws impairing the obligation of contracts and ex post facto laws, or any other provision of the particular constitution to which the legislature passing them may be subject. The purpose of these sections is merely to point out the effect, upon the construction of such, and acts declaratory of former statutes or rules of law, of the presumption against an intention to legislate retrospectively, and, possibly, of a constitutional prohibition against retrospective operation in the particular class of cases to which the act is to be applied, coupled with the necessity of giving, if practicable, a lawful and reasonable operation to the expression of the legislative will." (Endlich, Interpretation of Statutes, sec. 291.)

These principles apply, *mutatis mutandis*, to executive regulations. But it would be a violation of principles of a much higher degree of obligation, if they were to be resorted to in disregard of those mentioned in rule 4 and at the beginning of these remarks. Such a violation could not, indeed, be properly regarded as curative or declaratory.

8. The Army Regulations are, as the order of promulgation by the Secretary of War announces, "Regulations for the Army." Their provisions would not relate to the business of the War Department, unless it should expressly appear that such is the intention. Thus, it was held that paragraph 679, Army Regulations, only relates to the public property in the custody of the military establishment, and does not relate to the property held by the War Department proper, which is a civil institution, quite distinct from the military, and to which, in the absence of express words to that effect, the regulation mentioned does not apply. (Opin. Judge-Advocate General, January 10, 1898.)

9. Executive regulations are not in general imperative, so as to render actually invalid acts provided for by the regulations, but done without a compliance with their requirements. They are in general directory only. In this respect they resemble statutory rules for the performance of public duties. To affect with invalidity acts done in neglect of such rules would work serious general inconvenience or injustice to persons who have no control over those intrusted with the duty, without promoting the essential aims of the legislature. In such case, they are said not to be of the essence, or substance of the thing required; and, depending upon this quality of not being of the

essence or substance of the thing required, compliance being rather a matter of convenience, and the direction being given with a view simply to proper, orderly, and prompt conduct of business, they seem to be generally understood as mere instructions for the guidance and government of those on whom the duty is imposed, or, in other words, as directory only. (Endlich on Interpretation of Statutes, sec. 436.)

In general, statutes directing the mode of proceeding by public officers are deemed advisory, and strict compliance with their detailed provisions is not indispensable to the validity of the proceedings themselves, unless a contrary intention can be clearly gathered from the statute construed in the light of other rules of interpretation. (*Id.*, sec. 437.)

A provision in a statute, rule of procedure, or the like, is said to be directory when it is to be considered as a mere direction or instruction of no obligatory force, and involving no invalidating consequence for its disregard, as opposed to an imperative or mandatory provision which must be followed. The general rule is that the prescriptions of a statute relating to the performance of a public duty are so far directory that, though neglect of them may be punishable, yet it does not affect the validity of the acts done under them, as in the case of a statute requiring an officer to prepare and deliver a document to another officer on or before a certain day. (Black's Law Dictionary.)

Many statutory requisitions, intended for the guidance of officers in the conduct of business, do not limit their power or render its exercise in disregard of the requirements ineffectual. Such are regulations designed to secure order, system, and dispatch in proceedings. Provisions of this character are not mandatory unless accompanied by negative words importing that the acts shall not be done in any other manner or time than that designated. (Anderson's Law Dictionary.)

As with statutes, so with executive regulations, when it is the intention that acts shall be invalid unless done in the way prescribed, and therefore the way prescribed is of the essence of the regulation, the regulation is imperative, and not merely directory.

These rules have been applied in the construction of Army regulations. So held with reference to paragraph 746 of the Army Regulations of 1889, forbidding purchases of supplies to be made from, or contracts for supplies or services to be made with, persons in the military service, that it was directory merely, and that a contract might still be legal and binding, though entered into in contravention of its terms. (Dig. Opin. Judge-Advocate General, 296.) But a regulation which has been adopted by Congress, even though directory only, should not be deliberately set aside, any more than the directory requirements of a statute. Nor should a directory regulation made pursuant to or in aid of a statute be deliberately repudiated in an individual case. Such action would be unauthorized (and destructive to system), although the thing done would not thereby be rendered invalid. It has been held by the War Department that certain regulations made for the purpose of carrying out the law with reference to appointments from the ranks, and which prescribe requirements relating to the examination of candidates, can not be set aside in individual cases. This decision is manifestly correct, whether it rests on the ground that the regulations were intended to be imperative, or on the ground that the Department has no authority thus, in individual cases, to set aside regulations made pursuant to a statute, even though they be directory only.[1]

10. When there is a doubt as to the meaning of a regulation, reference may be had to the order, if any there be, on which it is based, for an explanation of the doubtful language. This is an application of a rule of statutory construction. Thus, Justice Miller, speaking of the Revised Statutes of the United States, said:

"Where there is a substantial doubt as to the meaning of the language used in the revision, the old law is a valuable source of information. The Revised Statutes must be treated as the legislative declaration of the statute law on the subjects which they embrace on the 1st day of December, 1873. When the meaning is plain, the courts can not look to the statutes which have been revised to see if Congress erred in that revision, but may do so when necessary to construe doubtful language used in expressing the meaning of Congress." (United States v. Bowen, 100 U. S., 513.)

So, where there is a doubt as to the meaning of a regulation, reference may be had to the antecedent history of the subject. This is not uncommonly a source of information in the construction of regulations, and recourse is often had to it as a matter of historical illustration and confirmation, even when the language of the regulation is entirely free from doubt.

---

[1] See G. C. M. O. No. 27, Navy Dep't, 1898.

11. "He knows not the law who knows not the reason for the law." In construing a regulation the reason for it may be taken into account, and cases excluded from it which, although within the letter of the regulation, are not within the reason for it. This also is the application of a principle of statutory construction. "It is a familiar rule," say the Supreme Court, "that a thing may be within the letter of the statute and yet not within the statute, because not within its spirit, nor within the intention of its makers. This has been often asserted, and the reports are full of cases illustrating its application. This is not the substitution of the will of the judge for that of the legislator, for frequently words of general meaning are used in a statute, words broad enough to include an act in question, and yet a consideration of the whole legislation, or of the circumstances surrounding its enactment, or of the absurd results which follow from giving such broad meaning to the words, makes it unreasonable to believe that the legislator intended to include the particular act."[1]

12. When the punctuation is such as to interfere with true interpretation, it should be disregarded. This rule of statutory interpretation is applicable to the interpretation of regulations. But the evidence of the interference should be clear. As stated by Black and the authorities cited by him: "In the interpretation of written instruments, very little consideration is given by the courts to the punctuation, and it is never allowed to interfere with or control the sense and meaning of the language used. The words employed must be given their common and

---

[1] 143 U. S., 459.

natural effect, regardless of the punctuation or grammatical construction; and considerations based on the punctuation alone must never be allowed to violate the well-settled rule that, where it is possible, effect must be given to every sentence, phrase, and word, and the parts must be compared and considered with reference to each other. Punctuation is a most fallible standard by which to interpret a writing; it may be resorted to when all other means fail; but the court will first take the instrument by its four corners, in order to ascertain its true meaning; if that is apparent on judicially inspecting the whole, the punctuation will not be suffered to change it.

"If, therefore, the words of the act, taken in themselves alone, or compared with the context and read in the light of the spirit and reason of the whole act, convey a precise and single meaning, they are not to be affected by the want of proper punctuation or by the insertion of incorrect or misplaced marks."[1]

"Punctuation in written instruments may sometimes, in cases of ambiguity, shed light upon the meaning of the parties, but it is never allowed to overturn what seems the plain meaning of the whole instrument. It may be resorted to when all other means fail."[2]

13. The Army Regulations consist of a great number of individual regulations, derived from a great variety of sources, and reduced to words by many different persons. They, to a large extent, relate to the business of the different staff departments of the Army, the regulations relating to one department

[1] Black's Construction and Interpretation of the Laws, p. 186.
[2] Am. and Engl. Enc. of Law, vol. II, p. 521, and authorities cited.

often not affecting others. Words may sometimes, in consequence of this, be differently used in different connections, or, perhaps, with meanings qualified by their surroundings. The rule of statutory construction, *Noscitur a sociis*, here applies. To illustrate: Paragraph 771, of the Army Regulations of 1889, prescribed that affidavits or depositions might be taken before certain military officers, without specifying in what cases. According to the language of this paragraph, taken by itself, these officers were given the power to take affidavits and depositions (which was held to include the administering of oaths) for all purposes whatsoever; but, as the paragraph was amongst other paragraphs, and in an article, relating to property accountability, it was evidently the intention to confer the power (an excess of authority even then) only for the purpose of accounting for public property in the custody of the military establishment. The meaning of the paragraph was determined by its surroundings.

14. As with statutes, so with executive regulations, contemporaneous construction, and official usage for a long period, by the persons charged with their administration, are among the legitimate aids in determining their meaning. By contemporaneous construction is meant that put on the regulation at the time that it was made. As usage under a regulation is generally founded on contemporaneous construction, these, thus united, should ordinarily be considered as conclusive; except, of course, when the question is as to a conflict between the regulation and some superior rule of action.¹

¹ Under the head of, "Principles governing Regulations," Colonel Winthrop, in his work on Military Law, points out and

In the administration of military affairs, as in other branches of government, precedents are of great value, and an authoritative construction, once given to a regulation, should thereafter receive great weight. *Stare decisis, et non quieta movere*, is a maxim applicable to constructions of regulations by the Executive, as well as to constructions of law by the courts. To change the accepted meaning of a regulation by a new construction is disturbing, and should be avoided. It is preferable to change the regulation itself when that can be done.

We see it sometimes announced that the action taken in a case will not be followed as a precedent. This is scarcely more than a declaration of a present intention in regard to future action, and as such affects only the authority making it, and is not even legally binding on him. If the thing done be within the legal power of the authority doing it, it will be a precedent, although, perhaps, weakened by the circumstances of the case. Accordingly, we find precedents of this kind cited, notwithstanding the announcement that the action taken is not to be so regarded.

But it is not the object of these remarks to treat the subject of the construction of regulations at any length. All that has been attempted has been to point out a few of the most important principles. For the rest it may be said that in general the rules of statutory construction will be safe guides.

---

discusses the following rules:
1. They must not contravene existing law.
2. They must not legislate.
3. They must confine themselves to their subject.
4. They must be uniform.
5. They should be equitable.

APPENDIX A.

LETTER OF THE SECRETARY OF WAR

IN REPLY TO

House Resolution of April 13, 1874, to examine and report on General Orders No. 32, War Department, Adjutant General's Office, of March 15, 1873, as published in Executive Document No. 275, House of Representatives, 43d Congress, 1st Session.

WAR DEPARTMENT, *June 1, 1874.*

SIR: Referring to the House resolution of April 13, 1874, to examine and report as to General Orders No. 32, War Department, Adjutant General's Office, of March 15, 1873, I inclose herewith a copy of that order.

In my annual report, which has been submitted to Congress, you will find specific reference to this order, with my reasons for issuing it.

The House resolution directs examination

1st. As to the authority of the Secretary of War to issue such order.

2d. Whether such order abridges the rights of officers in freedom of speech and to petition of Congress as citizens.

3. Whether such order is in contravention of exclusive right of Congress, under paragraph 13, section 8, Article VII of the Constitution, to make rules and regulations for the government of the Army, etc.

4th. As to the authority of the Secretary of War over retired officers who are not subject to assignment to any military duty.

I.

Under the first inquiry, as to my authority to issue the order, I have to say that it was issued by me under the authority intrusted by the President, under section 1 of the law of August

7, 1789, the orders of the Secretary of War (except as to duties specifically imposed by certain statutes) being, in contemplation of law, the orders of the President. (See Attorney-General Wirt's opinion of July 6, 1820.)

The United States Supreme Court has also ruled on this subject. In United States *v.* Eliason, 16 Pet., 291, the court said (p. 457, vol. 7):

"The Secretary of War is the regular constitutional organ of the President, for the administration of the military establishment of the nation; and rules and orders publicly promulged through him must be received as the acts of the Executive, and as such be binding upon all within the sphere of his legal and constitutional authority. Such regulations can not be questioned or defied, because they may be thought unwise or mistaken." (See also Wilcox *v.* Jackson, 13 Pet., 498.)

Such has been the uniform practice in the conduct of military affairs since the organization of the Army in 1790, and, if desired, this point could be greatly amplified and illustrated. (7 Opin. Atty. Gen., p. 453.)

II.

The second point of the resolution, as to whether such order abridges the right of officers in freedom of speech and the right to petition Congress as citizens of the United States under the Constitution, covers broader grounds.

Congress undoubtedly has unlimited power over the Army. Article I, section 8, gives it power "to raise and support armies," also, power "to make rules for the government and regulation of the land-forces;" and power "to make all laws which shall be necessary and proper for carrying into execution the foregoing powers, and all other powers vested by the Constitution in the Government of the United States, or any *department* or *officer* thereof."

Acting under this very extensive and unlimited power, Congress has raised and supported armies and provided statutory rules and articles for their governance, commonly known as the "Articles of War." (Act of April 10, 1806, and amendatory acts; see Scott's Digest United States Military Laws, p. 297.)

These, however, have formed but a statutory frame-work, as it were, because, in addition thereto, numerous regulations in aid or complement of the statutes (8 Opin. Atty. Gen., 343), as well as standing general orders for the government of the Army, have been issued by successive Executives.

Presidents Washington, Adams, and Jefferson, caused to be issued many such standing orders, from 1790 to 1819. (See Duane's Military Dictionary.)

Subsequently, Congress, by the acts of March 3, 1813, section 5, and April 24, 1816, section 9, gave specific power to the Secretary of War to make *general* regulations subject to approval of the President, which should be respected "and obeyed until altered or revoked by the same authority."

In discussing the "Navy Regulations," Attorney-General Cushing said (6 Opin., pp. 10, 15), that "cases may be supposed in which it is not easy to draw the line between what is legislative and what is executive or administrative, and so it is in regard to every such question of the distinction of powers."

He came to the conclusion that "the President and subordinate executive officers, whether military or civil, possess a limited power to establish regulations, provided these be in execution of, and supplemental to, the statutes and statute regulations; but not to repeal or contradict existing statutes or statute regulations, nor to make provisions of a legislative nature."

The difference between rules, regulations, and standing general orders is as follows:

"Rules" are *statutory* enactments for the government of the Army, affixing certain penalties for a violation, and declaring what shall be deemed military offenses. (See the "Rules and Articles of War," act of April 10, 1806.)

"General Regulations" are a system of ordinances for the administration of the affairs of the Army and for better defining and prescribing the respective duties and powers of officers and men in the military service, and embracing all necessary forms of a general character. (See acts March 3, 1813, section 5; July 28, 1866, section 37; July 15, 1870, section 20.)

Congress may make the regulations, or it may, as it has done, devolve on the President the authority to make regulations not inconsistent with law.

"Standing general orders" are *Executive* instructions, or directions to do or not to do particular acts.

Police and local or interior regulations come under this head. (See Duane's Military Dictionary; Army Regulations of 1821, approved for one year by Congress, and subject then remitted to President under acts of 1813 and 1816, article 5, par. 1, and article 36, par. 1.)

In Harvey *v.* United States, 3d Nott and Huntington's Rep., 42, the Court of Claims have held that a mere order of the President or of the Secretary of War is *not* regulation.

Article I of the amendments to the Constitution, declares that Congress shall make no law abridging the *freedom* of *speech* or the right of the *people* peaceably to assemble, and to petition the Government for a redress of grievances. This article, it is believed, is not in any way applicable to persons in the land forces, because *plenary* powers had already been given by the Constitution to Congress in respect to such persons, and article 10 of the amendments in saying that "powers not *delegated* to the United States by the Constitution * * * are reserved to the States, respectively, or to the people," contains the implication that the foregoing amendments had no reference whatever to the powers already delegated to Congress by the Constitution.

It seems further apparent that Article I of the amendments, just quoted, is not applicable to the Army from Article VI of the amendments, which provides that "in *all* criminal prosecutions the accused shall enjoy the right to a trial *by jury*, nor shall any person be subject for the same offense to be twice put in jeopardy of life or limb."

Despite this amendment soldiers are triable for crimes otherwise than by jury. (See sixty-fifth, sixty-sixth, and ninety-ninth articles of war.) Congress has, however, in the eighty-seventh article of war, declared that "no soldier shall be tried a second time for the same offense," which would hardly seem to have been necessary if the constitutional amendment was deemed applicable.

Article V of the amendments especially excepts criminal cases arising in the land forces from the necessity of presentment by the grand jury. Congress appears to have always acted on the views herein expressed.

Thus, in the Articles of War, there are numerous instances where Congress has abridged the freedom of speech, with reference to persons in the Army, by statutes not at all applicable to the people at large. (See articles 5, 23, 24, 28, 52, 53, and 57.)

The right of the *people* peacefully to assemble to petition the Government for a redress of grievances, is also a right incompatible with subordination and discipline in the military service.

A *citizen*, one of the people, as contradistinguished from a *soldier* in the amendments, can go where he pleases, provided he does not trespass; he can go to an assembly to make such petition.

The soldier has no such *right*. Congress, by the Articles of War, has limited and restricted his movements in numerous ways, dependent on the will of superior military authority. (See articles 12, 20, 21, 27, 44, 48, 50, and 52.)

It seems further apparent that this *right* of the *people* peaceably to assemble and petition the Government for a redress of *grievances* has no applicability to the military service, because Congress has provided, in the thirty-fourth and thirty-fifth articles of war (act of April 10, 1806), exactly how an officer or soldier may obtain redress of grievances, by an individual application through certain military channels. (See, also, general orders of September 24, 1806, from general headquarters.)

Should officers or soldiers endeavor to assemble, with a view of making a *joint* petition or application, such conduct would, under the article of war, be a military offense, triable, either as "sedition," under the seventh article of war, or as conduct to the prejudice of good order and military discipline, under the ninety-ninth article of war.

It would strike at the root of discipline and military subordination, so essential to the effectiveness of a military force, to concede that the Army could be turned into a debating society, to discuss the official acts of superior authority, on the plea that Article I of the constitutional amendments was paramount, and embraced such designated class of individuals. It would render nugatory the articles of war already recited, as well as that article (5) which makes the use of contemptuous or disrespectful words against the President, Vice-President, Congress, governor, or State legislature, an *offense*.

When the Pennsylvania and New Jersey lines, in 1781, respectively, undertook to proceed to places of assembly of their respective legislatures to obtain from the governor redress of grievances, the movement was not only seditious, but mutinous and dangerous to the safety of the nation, for the reason that these persons were not peaceful citizens, but armed and disciplined soldiers.

These preliminary observations are necessary, in order to show that the National Constitution nowhere gives any *right* to officers or soldiers in the Army, either as to freedom of speech or to petition Congress as citizens.

So long as such persons remain in the military service their *civil* rights are wholly subordinate to the will of Congress and the lawful orders of their proper military superiors; a citizen has the absolute right to vote in his own precinct after due residence, etc. A soldier has no such *right*, although he may have fulfilled all the requirements of the local statute. His superior officer may forbid him the privilege of going to the polls, and such prevention of the soldier from voting would not subject the officer to any punishment under the State law, because it would rest solely with him, under the laws of the United States, to determine what military necessity controlled his order.

Acting on these principles, Congress, by the ninety-ninth article of war, has made other proceedings military offenses besides those enumerated in such articles, because it declares that "all disorders and neglects which officers and soldiers may be guilty of, to the prejudice of good order and military discipline, *though not mentioned in the foregoing articles of war*, are to be taken cognizance of by a general or regimental court-martial, according to the nature and degree of the offense, and be punished at their discretion."

Under military law, it is held that a violation of a "standing general order" would necessarily fall under this article of war.

Under the heretofore unquestioned power vested in the President as Commander in Chief, and by the acts of Congress, many orders have been successively issued since 1790, restricting and controlling officers and soldiers in their movements and immunities. (See General Orders of May 22, 1797, from headquarters of the Army, Fort Washington.)

Notably are the orders as to how officers and soldiers shall wear their hair and beards. (See General Orders No. 31, Army Headquarters, Adjutant General's Office, June 12, 1851; General Orders No. 2, Army Headquarters, Adjutant General's Office, January 6, 1853.)

A hasty survey of past orders confirms these remarks.

On the subject of correspondence, General Orders No. 79, from the Adjutant General's Office, Washington, December 10, 1829, said:

"From the repeated attempts which have recently been made by officers of the Army to open a direct correspondence with the Department of War, and even with the Executive, on matters of military detail and points of duty, in disregard of the established rules of service, the General-in-Chief finds himself under the necessity of arresting the irregularity by calling the attention of those concerned to the directions contained in the sixty-sixth article of the General Regulations for the Army, on the subject of military correspondence. While a strict conformity to those directions is enjoined, a departure from them can be regarded only as a breach of military discipline, subjecting the offenders to the penalties provided by the Articles of War."

In the following year General Orders No. 18, April 20, 1830, from the same office, was issued. It said:

"From the number of letters referred to the general headquarters of the Army, addressed by soldiers to the Secretary of War, and to other members of the civil departments of the Government, asking to be discharged from the service, and in relation to other subjects—which letters ought to have been submitted, in the first instance, according to established rules, to their immediate commanding officers, and by them, if approved, to the colonels of their regiments, who would forward them through the proper channel of communication pointed out by the General Regulations—the major-general commanding the Army finds it his duty to put a stop to such irregularities, and to forbid them in future. In every case hereafter of a breach of the established rules of correspondence, the letters will be returned to the commanding officer, to be made the grounds of a charge of disobedience of orders, that the offenders may be brought to a court-martial to answer accordingly."

In 1837, General Orders No. 79, December 23, were issued from the Adjutant General's Office, Washington, in which Secretary of War Poinsett, in reenunciating the principle, said:

"Letters are frequently received at this Department, from officers of the Army, through members of Congress, preferring claims, or seeking redress of grievances, and too often couched in language disrespectful to their superiors in command. In such cases they will never be considered, however respectable the channel through which they come; but under no circumstances is it necessary for an officer to avail himself of any other than the regular military channel. Claims or remonstrances addressed to the Department in temperate and respectful language will be promptly considered, and decided on their merits without prejudice or partiality, according to the rules of equity or military usage, where it governs the case; and under no circumstances will such rules and usage be departed from, to favor or to wrong any one."

Coming down to 1861, Secretary of War Cameron, in General Orders No. 67, Adjutant General's Office, of August 26, ordered that—

* * * "All correspondence and communication, verbally or by writing, printing, or telegraphing, respecting operations of the Army or military movements on land or water, or respecting the troops, camps, arsenals, entrenchments, or military affairs, within the several military districts, by which intelligence shall be directly or indirectly given to the enemy, without the authority and sanction of the general in command, be, and the same are, absolutely prohibited, and from and after the date of this order, persons violating the same will be proceeded against under the fifty seventh article of war."

It is proper to remark that this was a time of war, but the authority to issue the order remains the same.

Later still, on March 30, 1864, the present Executive, then General in Chief, in General Orders 129, War Department, Adjutant General's Office, said:

"The attention of all officers is called to the Army Regulations and General Orders in regard to correspondence on official matters. All such correspondence must be conducted through the proper official channels, except in cases of pressing necessity, which do not leave time for regular communication, and then the necessity must be stated. All applications or correspondence, *through whomsoever made*, in violation of this order, will not be responded to, and the writers will be arrested and tried for disobedience of orders, or recommended to the President for dismissal."

The Constitution, section 2, paragraph 1, while making the President the Commander in Chief of the Army, has given him authority to require the opinion in writing of the principal officer in each of the Executive Departments, upon any subject relating to the duties of their respective offices; and section 3 says, "he shall from time to time give to Congress information of the state of the Union, and recommend to their consideration such measures as he shall judge necessary and expedient."

There is no law or constitutional provision giving like authority to any officer of the Army, constitutionally subordinate to the President, and it is reasonable to assume if such officers were entitled to such privilege, it would be stated in some such way.

The right of Congress, or of either House, collectively or by committee, to call on any officer of the Army for his advice or opinion on any matter is undoubted, because the Army is wholly the creation of Congress.

The endeavor of any officer or soldier, however, of his own motion, to address Congress or either House, or its Members, soliciting, suggesting, or recommending action by Members for or against military affairs concerning the "*whole* Army," is conceived to be a very different matter, liable to be detrimental to the public service and disrespectful to the President, with whom, officially, alone rests this power under the Constitution. General Orders No. 32 clearly expresses this opinion.

There are many instances where it becomes necessary for officers to apply to Congress for special bills of relief from liability for loss of public property for which accountable.

The order in question does not preclude any officer from making *direct* application to Congress, for the reason that the legislation applied for would be private and personal, as to the officer himself in an individual capacity, and not concerning the *whole* Army.

Occasionally it happens that an officer may make suggestions of great value to the service at large. This is provided for in the order by paragraph 2, which says that

"All petitions to Congress by officers, relative to subjects of a military character, will be forwarded through the General of the Army and Secretary of War for their action and transmittal."

From these observations is to be collected

1st. That no heretofore existing *right* of an officer in freedom of speech has been abridged by General Orders No. 32; and,

2d. That the only *right* to petition Congress being a right to petition for a redress of grievance, Congress has specifically provided in the Articles of War how an officer or soldier shall prefer such a petition and to whom. General Orders No. 32 does not apply to such matter.

As to the mere propriety or expediency of issuing this order, it is not believed any inquiry is intended.

III.

The third inquiry, whether such order is in contravention of the exclusive right of Congress, under the Constitution, to make rules for the government and regulation of the land forces, has already been answered under the second head, in discussing the difference between rules, regulations, and standing general orders.

In the case before cited of United States *v.* Eliason, the United States Supreme Court said (see also acts of Congress of March 3, 1813, and April 24, 1816, giving authority to make regulations):

"The power of the Executive to establish * * * regulations for the government of the Army is undoubted. The power to establish implies necessarily the power to modify or repeal, or to create anew.

* * * * * * *

"Such regulations can not be questioned or defied because they may be thought unwise or mistaken."

Again, in United States *v.* Freeman, 3 Howard's U. S. Rep., 566, the same court said that—

"The Army Regulations when sanctioned by the President have the force of law."

This was reaffirmed by the United States Supreme Court in Gratiot *v.* United States, 4 Howard's U. S. Rep., 80. General Orders No. 32 is, however, viewed as an Executive order rather than a regulation.

The before-quoted act of 1813 made it the *duty* of the Secretary of War, and authorized him, with the approval of the President, to prepare general regulations defining and prescribing the duties and powers of certain officers, and the act of April 24, 1816 (*ante*) recognized the regulations then in force, "subject, however, to such alterations as the Secretary of War may adopt, with the approbation of the President."

The law of July 28, 1866, section 37, enacted that the Secretary of War should submit to Congress on its next session a code of regulations * * *:

"The existing regulations to remain in force until Congress shall have acted on said report."

The action of Congress on that report was a negative one—in fact, no action at all; and in 1870 (act of July 15, section 20) Congress directed the Secretary of War to prepare a system of regulations, etc., which are now before it.

Whether section 37 of the above-recited act of July 28, 1866, *impliedly* repealed the old acts of 1813 and 1816, which gave to the President specific power to make regulations, is not necessary to be considered, in consequence of the light in which General Orders No. 32 is viewed, besides which the order does not modify any existing regulation.

Repeals by implication are never favored. Whenever Congress shall have prescribed a series of statutory regulations, there is no doubt that such regulations would then supersede and render nugatory any Executive regulations on the same subject.

Paragraph 3 of General Orders No. 32 refers to officers visiting Washington. A regulation of President Madison, of 1813, prescribed that—

"All officers arriving at the seat of Government will * * * report to the Adjutant-General."

The manner and mode of "reporting" is purely a subject of orders, liable to be changed according to circumstances. This, as well as authority to visit or remain at the seat of Government, has always been controlled or limited by the Executive or General-in-Chief acting under his authority, by general orders in the nature of local regulations.

The same authority to grant leaves of absence includes the power to prescribe the limits of such leaves.

Reference is made to annexed orders (marked A, B, C, and D), as showing the practice heretofore existing, where officers were even forbidden to visit Washington.

As General Orders No. 32 is in no way repugnant to, or in violation of, any statutory enactment, it is not perceived that it in any way contravenes the constitutional right of Congress to make rules and regulations for the government of the Army.

IV.

The fourth inquiry is as to the authority of the Secretary of War over officers of the Army *wholly* retired from active service and unassignable, under existing laws, to any kind of military duty.

There is some confusion of language in this part of the House resolution, so that the meaning is not readily discernible.

The law distinguishes between two classes of disabled officers:

First. Officers "partially retired," and

Second. Officers "wholly retired" from active service.

Over the latter class referred to in the resolution the President has no authority whatever.

The officer who is recommended by the retiring board to be "wholly retired from the service" ceases, on the approval of the President, connection with the military service. Under the statute he receives "one year's pay and allowances," and his name is "thenceforward omitted from the Army Register." (See act of Congress of August 3, 1861, section 17.)

If the House resolution was intended to refer not to "wholly retired officers," but to partially retired officers whose names are continued on the Army Register, I have to say that they are under military jurisdiction equally with other officers. Section 17 of the act of August 3, 1861, prescribed that such officers should be withdrawn from active service and command; but section 25 of the same act declared that—

"Retired officers of the Army * * may be assigned to such duties as the President may deem them capable of performing and such as the exigencies of the public service may require."

This section was modified (see act of January 21, 1870, section 1; resolution of April 6, 1870; act of July 15, 1870, section 23) so that now an officer on the retired list can be assigned to *duty* only at the "Soldiers' Home," or as professor in a college.

The following provision of law, with reference to such officers, is still in full force and effect. (Section 18, act of August 3, 1861.)

"The officers partially retired shall be entitled to wear the uniform of their respective grades; shall continue to be borne upon the Army Register * * * and shall be subject to the rules and articles of war, and to trial by general court-martial for any breach of the said articles."

Such officers are always required to report, by letter, monthly to the Adjutant General of the Army, and they are as liable to trial for disobedience of orders under the ninth article of war, such as failing, on direction, to report before a board of survey, as for any other breach of said articles.

It will be perceived that the retired list of the Army is very different from the pension list of the Interior Department, which is composed wholly of civilians not subject to military jurisdiction or to military law.

The War Department has recently been in receipt of applications from officers of the Army on the retired list, to practice as "claim-agents or attorneys," before the several Executive Departments of the Government. These officers are officers of the Government, holding places of profit and receiving 75 per cent. of the pay of the *rank* on which they are retired. (Act of July 15, 1870, section 24.)

In fact some of them, by being retired on the rank of the command in the volunteers held by them when wounded (act of July 28, 1866, section 32) receive now much more pay than while on the active list of the Army.

The act of February 26, 1853, section 2 (10 Stat., p. 170), strictly prohibits, under severe penalties, "any officer of the United States or person holding *any place* of trust or *profit* * * * under * * the Government," from acting as an agent or attorney to prosecute any claim against the United States, or in any manner or by any means, otherwise than in the discharge of proper official duties, aiding or assisting in the prosecution or support of any such claim.

The act of June 11, 1864, is also very explicit on this point. The act is as follows:

PUBLIC—No. 97.

AN ACT relating to members of Congress, heads of Departments, and other officers of the Government.

Be it enacted by the Senate and House of Representatives of the United States of America in Congress assembled, That no member of the Senate or House of Representatives shall, after his election and during his continuance in office, nor shall any head of a Department, head of a Bureau, clerk, or any other officer of the Government, receive, or agree to receive, any compensation whatsoever, directly or indirectly, for any services rendered, or to be rendered, after the passage of this act, to any person, either by himself or another, in relation to any proceeding, contract, claim, controversy, charge, accusation, arrest, or other matter or thing in which the United States is a party, or directly or indirectly interested, before any Department, court-martial, Bureau, officer, or any civil, military, or naval commission whatever. And any person offending against any provision of this act shall, on conviction thereof, be deemed guilty of a misdemeanor, and be punished by a fine not exceeding ten thousand dollars, and by imprisonment for a term not exceeding two years, at the discretion of the court trying the same, and shall be forever thereafter incapable of holding any office of honor, trust, or profit, under the Government of the United States.

Approved June 11, 1864.

(See also the equally positive act of July 13, 1866, section 62, chap. 184.)

In view of these explicit and peremptory laws this Department has invariably refused permission to any officer of the Army to act as agent or attorney for any individual, in the prosecution of any claim against the United States, or of any claim in which the United States is a party.

Very respectfully, your obedient servant,

WM. W. BELKNAP,
Secretary of War.

The SPEAKER *of the House of Representatives.*

[General Orders No. 32.]

WAR DEPARTMENT, ADJUTANT GENERAL'S OFFICE,
Washington, March 15, 1872.

The practice—which has prevailed to a considerable extent—of Army officers visiting and remaining at the seat of Government during the sessions of Congress, with the view of influencing legislation upon military affairs concerning the whole Army, and which have been or can be brought properly to the attention of Congress only by the President, the Secretary of War, or the General of the Army, has become a serious evil, highly detrimental to the public service and disrespectful to superior authority.

Such action on the part of Army officers not only consumes but is a task upon the time of members of Congress, causing them embarrassment and hindering necessary legislation—of which they justly complain—and injures the Army in public opinion. The advantages, if any, to the individual can not counteract the disadvantage to the service.

It is therefore ordered—

I. That no officer, either *active* or *retired*, shall, directly or indirectly, without being called upon by proper authority, solicit, suggest, or recommend action by members of Congress for or against military affairs.

The foregoing is not intended to preclude officers from illustrating or expounding a measure before Congress which may have received the favor or sanction of the President, Secretary of War, or General of the Army. The experience of officers when so used is and will be viewed as valuable.

II. All petitions to Congress by officers, relative to subjects of a military character, will be forwarded through the General of the Army and Secretary of War for their action and transmittal.

III. An officer visiting the seat of Government *during a congressional session* will, upon his arrival, register his name at the Adjutant General's Office, as now required, and, in addition, address a letter to the Adjutant General of the Army, reciting the purpose of and time that will be embraced by his visit, and the authority under which he is absent from his command or station. The purpose or object, so recited, will be the strict guide of the officer during his stay.

By order of the Secretary of War:

E. D. TOWNSEND,
Adjutant General.

A.

[Order No. 48.]

HEADQUARTERS OF THE ARMY,
ADJUTANT GENERAL'S OFFICE,
Washington, May 18, 1833.

The practice, which has so extensively prevailed, of the officers of the Army visiting the seat of Government, has been injurious to the public service. The evils of this practice have been not only in withdrawing officers from their proper stations, but frequently in its effects upon the business of the Army and upon public opinion.

There are no benefits to individuals which can counteract the disadvantages of this indiscriminate indulgence.

Where such visits are necessary for the public service, or for any just right of the individual concerned, they will be authorized.

Nor will reasonable indulgence for the gratification of a laudable curiosity be refused where the circumstances of the applicants make those proper, and where the public interest will not suffer.

But of the propriety of these the General-in-Chief will judge, and, therefore, no officer will visit the seat of Government unless ordered, or unless specially permitted so to do by the General-in-Chief.

An officer, however, may pass through the seat of Government when on duty or on a leave of absence, provided it is the most direct route to his place of destination; but in such case he will report in person to the Adjutant General, and will not remain more than twenty-four hours.

* * * * * * *

By order of Major General Macomb:

R. JONES,
Adjutant General.

B.

[Order No. 79.]

HEADQUARTERS OF THE ARMY,
ADJUTANT GENERAL'S OFFICE,
Washington, September 30, 1835.

The regulation of the War Department, promulgated to the Army in order No. 48, has been modified according to the following direction of the Secretary of War:

DEPARTMENT OF WAR, *September 30, 1835.*

That part of the regulation quoted in Order No. 48, which prohibited the officers of the Army from visiting the seat of Government without express permission, was adopted with a view to prevent the recurrence of difficulties, which had frequently been experienced in the administration of the concerns of the Army. It was not intended to impair the just rights or reasonable expectations of the officers, still less to affect that pride of character, personal and professional, which has always been cherished in the American Army, and without which their country would have little to expect from their services.

The limitation imposed by the same regulation, upon the practice of granting leave of absence, will have a tendency to diminish much of the evil which the above prohibition was intended to obviate. And should experience hereafter show that its operation is still so injurious as to require further remedy, while such remedy will be applied so as best to attain the object, it will be applied with every just regard to the honor and feelings of the officer.

Under these circumstances, therefore, paragraph No. 7, under the head of "Leaves of absence," of the regulation above referred to, is hereby rescinded.

LEW. CASS.

By order of Major General Macomb:

R. JONES,
Adjutant General.

C.

[General Orders No. 114.]

WAR DEPARTMENT, ADJUTANT GENERAL'S OFFICE,
Washington, August 21, 1862.

1. No officer of the Regular Army or of volunteers will hereafter visit the city of Washington without special permission. Leaves of absence will not be considered as including the city of Washington, unless so stated, and leaves for that purpose can only be given by the authority of the War Department, through the Adjutant General.

II. Officers on leave of absence will not leave the limits of their military department without special permission.

By order of the Secretary of War:

E. D. TOWNSEND,
Assistant Adjutant General.

D.

[General Orders No. 31.]

WAR DEPARTMENT, ADJUTANT GENERAL'S OFFICE,
Washington, May 18, 1866.

Officers permitted to visit Washington when on leave.

General Orders No. 114, dated War Department, Adjutant General's Office, Washington, August 21, 1862, prohibiting officers on leave of absence from visiting Washington without special permission, is hereby rescinded.

The attention of all officers arriving at the seat of Government is directed to the regulation requiring them to report at the office of the Adjutant General, and record their names and residence in the city.

By order of the Secretary of War:

E. D. TOWNSEND,
Assistant Adjutant General.

APPENDIX B.

EXTRACT FROM THE JUDGE-ADVOCATE GENERAL'S REMARKS ON REVOCABLE LICENSES.

The foregoing remarks are taken from a discussion on the source of authority of the Army regulations, but they apply as well to the power of granting revocable licenses. As is pointed out in that discussion, the power to make Army regulations rests primarily with Congress, under its constitutional power, "To make rules for the government and regulation of the land and naval forces." Nevertheless, as repeatedly declared by the Supreme Court, the President has also the power to make Army regulations, and regulations so made have the force of law. (United States *v.* Freeman, 3 How., 567; Gratiot *v.* United States, 4 How., 118; United States *v.* Eliason, 16 Pet., 302; Kurtz *v.* Moffitt, 115 U. S., 503.)

As also stated in the discussion referred to, Congress might, *if it were practicable*, cover by its legislation the whole field of Army regulations, and leave nothing to the President, because the power rests *primarily* with Congress. But it is not practicable.

So the Constitution prescribes that "The Congress shall have power to dispose of and make all needful rules and regulations respecting the territory or other property belonging to the United States." Were it practicable, Congress could cover this whole field also, and leave nothing to the President. But it is not practicable.

"From an early period in the history of the Government," said the Supreme Court in Grisar *v.* McDowell, "it has been the practice of the President to order, from time to time, as the exigencies of the public service required, parcels of land belonging to the United States to be reserved from sale and set apart for public uses"—in the exercise of that general power, which the court more fully considered in the Neagle case. This is an exercise of a power which, in the first instance, is clearly vested in Congress; but, in the absence of the exercise of jurisdiction over the subject matter by Congress, it is legal, because it is an exercise of a power included in the President's power as Executive, to "take care that the laws be faithfully executed." Can it be said that the power of the President extends to the setting aside of lands for public purposes, and yet not to the making of reasonable regulations regarding them while they are under his charge?

Now, when the land is set apart for a military purpose, necessities for giving permissions of different kinds arise—principally relating to the requirements and convenience of the residents on the reservation; and, in so far as such permissions do no injury to the property of the United States, the power of the President to grant them has not been questioned.

It is on the face of it impossible for Congress to provide by legislation for every case which may arise, because unforeseen necessities for permissions of various kinds, often needing immediate action, spring up, and these can only be met by an exercise of the power of the Executive. These permissions are not always granted by formal written licenses. They may not be reduced to writing at all, but be entirely informal, oral permissions, to do acts which without them would constitute trespass. These are in effect and substance revocable licenses, just as much as those expressed in a written instrument. Indeed, the great mass of licenses to do acts of various kinds on military reservations are informal permissions of this character. Whether it be to enjoy some continuous privilege or to do a single act, makes no difference. All are in effect revocable licenses, emanating from the same authority. And the only advantage of the revocable license by written instrument is that it is the most convenient evidence of the permission. Many acts are, however, such that it would be absurd to resort to written instruments for the purpose of granting permission to do them. They are simply orally authorized or silently permitted, the authority being the authority of the President, executed through the commanding officer of the post. At every large post there are, no doubt, a great number of such acts done daily by the authority of these unwritten permissions, or unwritten revocable licenses.

The power of the President probably does not extend to the granting of licenses for the doing of anything which would be an injury to the property, nor can he grant other than revocable permissions, but there appear to be no other restrictions. He can not grant licenses that are not revocable, so that if it be for the erection of a building, whether it be of stone or wood is immaterial; in either case the license must be revocable. The power is one to be exercised by the President at his discretion, subject only to the restrictions mentioned, and of course to such other restrictions as may be imposed by or be the result of acts of Congress. The act of July 28, 1892, authorizing the Secretary of War to grant leases, seems to have been intended as an extension, certainly not as a restriction, of his power. It is inapplicable to the purposes for which revocable licenses are used. And the sixth section of the act of July 5, 1884, "to provide for the disposal of abandoned and useless military reservations," authorizing the Secretary of War to permit the extension of roads across military reservations, the landing of ferries and the erection of bridges thereon, and to permit cattle to be driven across them, was apparently intended to confer power on him to grant more permanent privileges than revocable licenses give.

A license is a bare authority to do a certain act or series of acts upon the land of the licensor without possessing or acquiring any estate therein. The Judge-Advocate General's Office has always held that the Secretary of War may, by revocable license, permit a temporary use, terminable at his discretion, as the public interests may require, of United States lands under his control, provided such license conveys no usufructuary interest in the land, and such use does not conflict with the purpose for which the land is held. (See Dig. Opin. Judge-Advocate General, p. 476.) "The word license, as applied to real property, imports an authority to do some act or series of acts upon the land of another. It passes no interest in the land itself and its only effect is to legalize an act which in the absence of the license would constitute a trespass. It may be created by parol, although a writing defining the exact nature and scope of the license is preferable." (Rice on Real Property, p. 505.)

In 1891 the Secretary of War decided that military reservations and lands occupied by the War Department are held and occupied for military purposes only, and that no licenses for their use or occupation would be given without authority from Congress, unless such use or occupation would be of some benefit to the military service. (Circ. 12, Hdqr. of the Army.) It will be noticed that this is merely the announcement of a policy, and not the denial of the existence of the power. And, as a matter of fact, the policy thus declared, was not carried out. In practice it is fully recognized that the Secretary of War may thus license any act which would not be an injury to the property, nor conflict with the purpose for which it is held. This, it is believed, is giving a reasonable application to the rule against the granting of usufructuary interests or permission to commit waste. In a recent case, where the question was whether the Secretary of War had authority to permit the removal of sand, it was said: "It has heretofore been held by this Office (the Judge-Advocate General's) that the Secretary of War has no authority to grant a usufructuary interest in lands of the United States, and it might be said that he has no authority to permit waste, i. e., a material alteration or deterioration of the freehold. I am inclined to believe that a safe view to take in this case is that, in the absence of any legislation on the subject, a revocable license may be granted, provided the act to be licensed would not be an injury to the property."

In 1890 the following question was submitted to the Attorney-General:

"Has the Secretary of War the legal authority to grant a license, revocable at the pleasure of the Secretary of War, to construct and maintain an irrigating ditch through a United States military reservation?"

The Attorney-General held:

"It has been the practice for many years for the Secretary of War, and sometimes the President, as the files of your Department will no doubt show, to grant revocable licenses to individuals to enter upon military reservations and prosecute undertakings there which may be beneficial to the military branch of the public service as well as advantageous to the licensees.

"For many years a part of the tracks of the Baltimore and Ohio Railroad Company was laid by a revocable license on a part of the land at Harper's Ferry used by the United States for a manufactory of arms. Under a similar license a part of the land belonging to the fort at Old Point Comfort was allowed to be used as a site for a hotel, and in 1864 President Lincoln gave a license of this kind to a railroad company to use a part of the

Government land at Sandy Hook, and in 1869 another license was granted to said company to use part of the same land 'so long as it may be considered expedient and for the public interest by the Secretary of War, or other proper officer of the Government, in charge of the United States lands at Sandy Hook.' (See 16 Opin., 212.)

"In this case the license applied for relates to a military reservation situated in an arid region, and therefore, in view of the advantage to Fort Selden of the use of this water, and in view of the frequent exercise of a similar power by granting such licenses as occasions have arisen through so many years, it seems clear that such license may be granted, the same to be under well-considered restrictions, and revocable at the will and pleasure of the Secretary of War."

In the joint resolution introduced by Mr. Fenton, at the second session of the Fifty-fourth Congress, "relative to the practice of granting permits for the occupancy or use of military reservations for non-military purposes," and referred to the Committee on Military Affairs of the House of Representatives, but not reported, there was this recital: "Whereas in the absence of specific legislation relating thereto, the custom has gradually obtained, in the War Department, of granting 'revocable licenses,' permitting citizens to occupy or use military reservations for personal or non-military purposes." But, as we have seen, the granting of these licenses rests on higher authority than the custom of the War Department.

And it may be added, on the strength of a decision of the Supreme Court in Benson *v.* United States, 146 U. S., 325, that the temporary appropriation of a locality on a military reservation to a non-military purpose does not have the effect of a diversion of the reservation from the purpose for which it is held. In that case Mr. Justice Brewer said, that the entire tract in question having been legally reserved for military purposes, and the character and purposes of its occupation having been officially and legally established by that branch of the Government which has control over such matters, it is not open to the courts, on a question of jurisdiction, to inquire what may be the actual uses to which any portion of the reserve is temporarily put.

The object of the joint resolution mentioned was to make it unlawful "to issue a license or permit to any religious denomination or sect to erect, or to exclusively occupy, a church edifice or chapel for sectarian purposes on any military reservation of the United States," and to require the Secretary of War to revoke all such licenses already granted.

Of course such action would be entirely within the power of Congress. Congress has absolute control over the matter. All that is claimed is, that when Congress does not act the President has power to act. So far as regards the "sectarian purpose" for which a license may be required, it is evident that such purpose does not affect the power to grant the license, but the policy of granting it only. In the absence of action by Congress, the exercise of the power rests in the discretion of the President, and the purpose can be no restriction on his discretion, except in so far that it must not be incompatible with, that is, an interference with or an obstruction to, the general use for which the land is held.[1]

[1] But see opinion of Attorney General of May 19, 1897, in which it is said: "West Point is Government property, and hence conveyances of it or uses of it can only be authorized by Congress." This, however, has not been given general effect.

November 11, 1897, the War Department issued the following:

REGULATIONS GOVERNING THE USE AND OCCUPATION OF LANDS WITHIN THE LIMITS OF THE MILITARY RESERVATION OF FORT ST. MICHAEL, ALASKA.

WAR DEPARTMENT, *Washington, October 20, 1897.*

1. By authority of the President, the land known as St. Michael Island, Alaska, with all contiguous land and islands within one hundred miles of the location of the flagstaff of the present garrison on that island, is set aside from the public lands of the Territory of Alaska and declared a military reservation.

Parties who have, prior to the receipt of this order, located and erected buildings on the land so reserved, will not be disturbed in their use of lands, buildings, and improvements, nor in the erection of structures needed for their business or residence.

2. The military reservation above declared, and the military post located thereon, will be known as *Fort St. Michael*, and will be under the control and supervision of the commanding officer of the troops there stationed.

R. A. ALGER,
Secretary of War.

In the absence of other provision of law and of all local civil officials within the limits of country surrounding the island of St. Michael, and the mouth of the Yukon River, the foregoing described reservation has been established for the security of life and property, the preservation of order, and the protection of property and business interests. Proper persons, associations, or corporations already located on, or desiring to enter upon and conduct legitimate business enterprises within the limits of this military reservation, will observe the following regulations:

1. Applications for permission must be accompanied by testimonials of good character and standing and be made in writing, addressed to the Secretary of War, reciting the nature of the business to be conducted; the location, as nearly as possible, on unoccupied land within the reservation; the area of land necessary; number and character of buildings, etc., to be erected, and probable date when occupancy is to be commenced and terminated. Those located on this reservation at the time the reservation was made will in like manner present their application for permits, and the commanding officer will not disturb them in their use and occupancy in conformity to these regulations until the action of the Secretary of War on their application is known.

2. The permit to be issued by the Secretary of War will describe the persons, business, location, etc., and will authorize the grantees to enter upon the reservation at the location named, and maintain the specified business, and *none other.* Where a definite location can not be given in the permit, authority will be given to the commanding officer of Fort St. Michael to authorize an appropriate location; but no permission will be given to use land that was included under the original order as located and used, and no permit will be given to locate on the land set apart for buildings, wharves, parade, and drill grounds for the post of Fort St. Michael. A plat showing authorized locations and grounds, with the name or names of the holders of permits, will be kept in the office of the commanding officer.

3. This permit will not be negotiable and will be of no value or effect until presented to and recorded by the commanding officer of Fort St. Michael, and the location staked out by him. It will not be transferable without the approval of the Secretary of War, except where both parties to the transfer are on the ground and one desires to dispose of his interest, in which event the commanding officer of Fort St. Michael may authorize the transfer, reporting his action to the War Department. It will give no right or title to ownership of lands occupied and is revocable at the will of the Secretary of War.

4. Applications for permission to sell any improvements made through virtue of these permits must be made through the commanding officer of Fort St. Michael to the Secretary of War and will only be approved on the same conditions on which a permit is originally issued.

5. Persons, associations, or corporations occupying lands, buildings, or privileges under these permits will be subject at all times to such police regulations as may be imposed from time to time by the commanding officer of Fort St. Michael or higher authority.

6. Any modification of this permit, after use, must be applied for in writing, and forwarded through the commanding officer of Fort St. Michael for the action of the Secretary of War; notice of a proposed termination of the permit will be given by the grantee at least thirty days before removal, and upon removal from the reservation the permit will be surrendered to the commanding officer of Fort St. Michael; and the location must be left by the occupants in good sanitary and police condition.

7. In case of naturally restricted landings, sites for buildings, ship-yards, etc., no monopoly will be given to any person or corporation, and no permit will be construed to do this, and all disagreements between holders of permits will, after a careful hearing by him, be settled by the commanding officer of Fort St. Michael.

8. No retail of distilled spirits on the reservation will be allowed; but this prohibition shall not include light wines or beer. (Section 1955, Revised Statutes; act approved May 17, 1884.)

9. It is to be understood that these permits are issued subject to any subsequent legislation of Congress.

APPENDIX C.

EXTRACT FROM THE OPINION OF HON. J. M. DICKINSON, ACTING ATTORNEY-GENERAL,

WITH REFERENCE TO THE

Constitutionality of the Act of Congress giving to the Secretary of War certain powers in regard to unreasonable obstructions to navigation.

In this case the Secretary of War is made a special tribunal to adjudicate facts.

It is competent for the legislature to establish, independent of the courts, special tribunals whose judgment shall be final.

The taxing interests of this country involve by far the largest question so far as value is concerned. The assessment of property is necessarily intrusted to special tribunals, which operate constantly and upon a vast scale. They are composed of nonjudicial officers, and if they pursue the law their conclusions are final.

In Nishimura Ekiu v. United States, 142 U. S., 651, and Fong Yue Ting v. United States, 149 U. S., 698, and Lem Moon Sing v. United States, 158 U. S., 538, it was held that Congress might intrust to executive officers the final determination of facts upon which foreigners might be sent out of or excluded from this country, and that their conclusions could not be reexamined by any court.

Congress has repeatedly passed laws committing the execution of acts in regard to the admission of aliens into the United States to the Secretary of the Treasury, collectors of customs, and to inspectors acting under their authority. (See acts of March 3, 1875, chapter 141 (18 Stat., 477); August 3, 1882, chapter 376 (22 Stat., 214); February 23, 1887, chapter 220 (24 Stat., 414); October 19, 1888, chapter 1210 (25 Stat., 566).)

By section 3, 22 Stat., 214, and in similar laws, the Secretary of the Treasury was authorized to establish rules and regulations and to issue instructions to carry out these and other immigration laws of the United States.

In Enterprise Saving Association v. Zumstein, 67 Fed. Rep., 1000, it was held by the circuit court of appeals of the sixth circuit, in an opinion delivered by Judge Lurton, and concurred in by Judges Taft and Severens, that in enforcing the postal laws against lotteries it was competent for Congress to intrust to the head of the Post Office Department the determination of the question as to what was a lottery.

Congress can only legislate in a general way, and large powers are necessarily intrusted to the different departments—such, for instance, as the supervising power given to the Secretary of the Interior over questions of patents and relations to Indians and the public lands. It has been held that he can set aside a survey and order another survey and issue a patent thereon, which is the exercise of judicial power. This right arises from the supervising power given him under the statute, and the courts have invariably sustained it, and in speaking of this class of powers have said:

"It is obvious, it is common knowledge, that in the administration of such large and varied interests as are intrusted to the Land Department, matters not foreseen, equities not anticipated, and which are, therefore, not provided for by express statute, may sometimes arise, and, therefore, that the Secretary of the Interior is given that superintending and supervising power which will enable him, in the face of these unexpected contingencies, to do justice." (Williams v. United States, 138 U. S., 524; Knight v. United States Land Assn., 142 U. S., 181.)

In McCulloch v. Maryland, 4 Wheat., 316, 421, Chief Justice Marshall said:

"The sound construction of the Constitution must allow to the National Legislature that discretion, with respect to the means by which the powers it confers are to be carried into execution, which will enable that body to perform the high duties assigned to it in the manner most beneficial to the people. Let the end be legitimate, let it be within the scope of the Constitution, and all means which are appropriate, which are plainly adapted to that end, which are not prohibited but consist with the letter and spirit of the Constitution, are constitutional."

It has now been established beyond controversy that Congress has the power to incorporate national banks and clothe them with large discretionary powers and for the purpose of accomplishing what Congress itself might directly do.

This power was maintained in McCulloch v. Maryland, 4 Wheat., 316, and in Osborn v. United States Bank, 9 Wheat., 738, mainly upon the ground that it was an appropriate means for carrying on the money transactions of the Government. (Legal Tender Case, 110 U. S., 415.)

In re The Laura, 114 U. S., 411, although the pardoning power is, by the Constitution, vested in the President, the court held that an act authorizing the Secretary of the Treasury to remit fines and penalties incurred by a steam vessel was valid, and it held that to determine otherwise would be to overthrow the practice which had been observed and acquiesced in for nearly a century.

In Dorsheimer v. United States, 7 Wall., 166, it was held that such power intrusted to the Secretary of the Treasury is one for the exercise of his discretion in a matter intrusted to him alone, and that it admits of no appeal to any court.

In all those cases in which it is held that executive officers of the Government will not be controlled by the court in matters in which they have to exercise judgment or discretion, it is apparent that large powers are intrusted by Congress under the acts investing them with authority, and that they really exercise in this way, by delegation, and necessarily so, for the purpose of carrying on the vast affairs of the Government and its details, authority which in a strict sense pertains to Congress. (See Decatur v. Paulding, 14 Pet., 497 514; United States v. Guthrie, 17 How., 284; United States v. The Commissioners, 5 Wall., 563; Litchfield v. Register and Receiver, 9 Wall., 575-577; Carrick v. Lamar, 116 U. S., 426.)

In United States v. Breen, 40 Fed. Rep., 402, it was held that Congress can authorize the Secretary of War to make rules and regulations, and can make it a misdemeanor to violate these rules when so made.

In United States v. Bailey, 9 Pet., 238, it was held that the crime of perjury, which was defined by statute, could be com-

mitted by taking an oath in conformity with a mere regulation of the Treasury Department.

In Caha v. United States, 152 U. S., 219, in commenting upon this decision, the court said:

"It was held that the Secretary had power to establish the regulation, and that the effect of it was to make the false affidavit before the justice of the peace perjury within the scope of the statute, and this notwithstanding the fact that such justice of the peace was not an officer of the United States."

In the Caha case, the court upheld an indictment for perjury, which grew out of proceedings instituted in accordance with regulations of the Interior Department.

These cases and the case under consideration differ from that of United States v. Eaton, 144 U. S., 677, in which the court held that a failure to comply with regulations made by the Commissioner of Internal Revenue could not be punished. The reason was that the statute had not made such refusal an offense.

The court said:

"It is necessary that a sufficient statutory authority should exist for declaring any act or omission a criminal offense; and we do not think that the statutory authority in the present case is sufficient. If Congress intended to make it an offense for wholesale dealers in oleomargarine to omit to keep books and render returns, as required by regulations to be made by the Commissioner of Internal Revenue, it would have done so distinctly, in connection with an enactment such as that above recited, made in section 41 of the act of October 1, 1890.

"Regulations prescribed by the President and by the heads of departments, under authority granted by Congress, may be regulations prescribed by law, so as lawfully to support acts done under them and in accordance with them, and may thus have, in a proper sense, the force of law; but it does not follow that a thing required by them is a thing so required by law as to make the neglect to do the thing a criminal offense in a citizen where a statute does not distinctly make the neglect in question a criminal offense." (p. 688.)

The case under discussion has the element which was lacking in the Eaton case, for a statute has distinctly made the neglect in question a misdemeanor.

The act of July 5, 1884, section 3, makes the Commissioner of Navigation's finding conclusive on all questions of interpretation growing out of the execution of the laws relating to the collection of tonnage tax. (N. G. L. S. S. Co. *v.* Hedden, 43 Fed. Rep., 17–25.)

Among the powers conferred upon Congress by the eighth section of the first article of the Constitution are the following:

To provide and maintain a navy.

To make rules for the government and regulation of the land and naval forces.

It was held in Dynes *v.* Hoover, 18 How., 20, and the decision has never been questioned, that, under this provision of the Constitution, Congress has the authority to establish courts-martial.

It was further held that the decision of the court martial in a matter where it has jurisdiction is final and can not be reviewed by the courts. (20 How., 83; Johnson *v.* Sayre, 158 U. S., 109.)

Congress, in establishing courts-martial, provided that the Secretary of the Navy is authorized to establish "regulations of the Navy," with the approval of the President. (12 Stat., 565; sec. 1547, Rev. Stat.)

Pursuant to this authority "regulations for the administration of law and justice" were issued on the 15th of April, 1870.

It has been held that such regulations have the force of law. (Gratiot *v.* United States, 4 How., 80; *Ex parte* Reed, 100 U. S., 22.)

Thus the legislative power is not exercised in detail, but a court is established in pursuance of the power conferred upon Congress, and the Secretary of the Navy is clothed with the power of making regulations to control the court.

This is one of the many instances in which it is essential for the operations of a great Government that matters of detail be intrusted by the legislative department to executive officers for the purpose of giving effect to legislative acts.

By article 34, Revised Statutes, section 1624, the proceedings of summary courts martial are to be conducted under such forms and rules as may be prescribed by the Secretary of the Navy, with the approval of the President.

Here Congress has constituted a court and it has delegated to an executive officer authority to establish rules for its procedure.

By section 1547, Revised Statutes, the regulations issued by the Secretary of the Navy, and as they might thereafter be altered by him, with the approval of the President, are recognized as the regulations of the Navy.

In pursuance of these regulations Sayre became "a person in the naval service of the United States." He was tried by a court martial, and the Supreme Court refused to review its findings. (Johnson v. Sayre, 158 U. S., 117.)

By an act of June 23, 1874 (18 Stat. L., 237, 240), an appropriation was made to be expended under the direction of the Secretary of War for the repairs, preservation, and completion of certain public works and *inter alia* "for the improvement of the harbor of Savannah."

A like appropriation was made by the act of March 3, 1875 (18 Stat., 459), "for the improvement of the harbor of Savannah, Ga."

Neither of these acts directed the manner in which these appropriations should be expended. The mode of improving the harbor was left to the discretion of the Secretary of War.

The legislative department declared that the improvement should be made, and devolved the determination of what would or would not be an improvement upon the Secretary of War.

It was contended that, while Congress had the power to authorize the construction of a specific work, it could not invest the Secretary of War with such large discretion, and that for this reason the act was void. The Supreme Court sustained the act in South Carolina v. Georgia, 93 U. S., 13.

In that case, acting under the commerce clause, Congress authorized an improvement. It empowered the Secretary of War to determine what would or would not be an improvement, and so the act could not be made effective without the action of the Secretary of War. If he determined the character of the improvement, that was final and the act operated upon it.

In this case, Congress makes the obstruction to navigation a misdemeanor. It devolves upon the Secretary of War to determine when there is an obstruction and to give the party a hearing upon the investigation. When this special tribunal has determined that there is an obstruction, then the act operates upon it as in the former case.

In Miller v. Mayor of New York, 109 U. S., 385, 393, 395, it appeared that Congress authorized the building of a bridge over a river, but the particular bridge authorized was such as should thereafter be approved by the Secretary of War. After the Secretary of War fixed by his approval the character of the bridge which was not an obstruction to navigation, then the act operated upon it and authorized the building of the bridge. Until then the legislative license did not go into effect. Here was a complete act in the abstract, but its operation in the concrete was dependent upon the determination of facts by the special tribunal. It was contended that this was an unlawful delegation of the power vested in Congress. The court held to the contrary, saying:

"By submitting the matter to the Secretary, Congress did not abdicate any of its authority to determine what should or should not be deemed an obstruction to the navigation of the river. It simply declared that, upon a certain fact being established, the bridge should be deemed a lawful structure, and employed the Secretary of War as an agent to ascertain that fact. Having power to regulate commerce with foreign nations and among the several States, and navigation being a branch of that commerce, it has the control of all navigable waters between the States, or connecting with the ocean, so as to preserve and protect their free navigation. Its power, therefore, to determine what shall not be deemed, so far as that commerce is concerned, an obstruction, is necessarily paramount and conclusive. It may in direct terms declare absolutely, or on conditions, that a bridge of a particular height shall not be deemed such an obstruction; and, in the latter case, make its declaration take effect when those conditions are complied with. The act in question, in requiring the approval of the Secretary before the construction of the bridge was permitted, was not essentially different from a great mass of legislation directing certain measures to be taken upon the happening of particular contingencies or the ascertainment of particular information. The execution of a vast number of measures authorized by Congress, and carried out under the direction of heads of departments, would be defeated if such were not the case. The efficiency of an act as a declaration of legislative will must, of course, come from Congress, but the ascertainment of the contingency upon which the act shall take effect may be left to such agencies as it may designate." (South Carolina v. Georgia, 93 U. S., 13.)

By section 2380, Revised Statutes —

"The President is authorized to reserve from the public lands, whether surveyed or unsurveyed, town sites on the shores of harbors, at the junction of rivers, important portages, or any natural or prospective centers of population."

Following strict construction this would be a delegation by Congress of its legislative power.

In Currier v. West Side Elevated Patent Ry. Co., 6 Blatch., 187, it was held that authority conferred upon commissioners to approve an experimental elevated railroad, and making such approval essential to the continuance in existence of the railroad, was not a delegation of legislative power.

The creation of a railroad commission to fix reasonable tolls for freight and passenger transportation is not an unconstitutional delegation of legislative powers. (Georgia v. Smith, 70 Ga., 694.)

Neither is giving power to the governor to make pilotage regulations. (Martin v. Witherspoon, 135 Mass., 175.)

The statute providing for the civil service authorizes the Commissioners and the President to make rules for carrying the act into effect, and the President is authorized to prescribe such regulations for the admission of persons into the civil service of the United States as may best promote the efficiency thereof. (22 Stat., 403; sec. 1753, Rev. Stat.)

Under the act of February 8, 1887 (24 Stat., 388), power is conferred upon the President, when he shall have determined certain facts, to allot land in severalty to Indians on reservations.

In Field v. Clark, 143 U. S., 649, it was held that Congress might confer authority upon the President to suspend by proclamation the operation of the law, affecting the importation of certain articles, upon his determination that any country producing such articles imposed duties upon the agricultural or other products of the United States which, in his opinion, were reciprocally unequal or unreasonable.

The court said:

"Legislative power was exercised when Congress declared that the suspension should take effect upon a named contingency.

What the President was required to do was simply in execution of the act of Congress. It was not the making of law. He was the mere agent of the law-making department to ascertain and declare the event upon which its expressed will was to take effect." (p. 693.)

I am of the opinion that the sections in question are not an unconstitutional delegation of the legislative function.

APPENDIX D.

EXTRACT FROM THE REGULATIONS FOR THE GOVERNMENT OF THE REVENUE CUTTER SERVICE.

ADMINISTRATION AND DISCIPLINE.

Exercise of Authority.

681. All persons in the Revenue-Cutter Service are required and strictly enjoined to properly observe and obey the lawful orders of their superiors, and to use their utmost exertions to carry such orders into effect with promptitude and zeal. They shall show to their superiors all proper deference and respect.

682. Superiors of every grade are forbidden to oppress or maltreat those under their command by tyrannical or capricious conduct, or abusive language. Authority over subordinates will be exercised with firmness, kindness, and justice, and each person shall set an example of morality and devotion to duty.

683. Punishments shall be in strict conformity to law and in accordance with the usages of the sea service, and will follow the offense as promptly as circumstances will permit.

684. In order to avoid unnecessary recourse to boards of investigation, it is directed that when an officer shall be reported for grave misconduct to his immediate commanding officer the latter shall institute a careful inquiry into the circumstances on which the complaint is founded. To this end he shall call upon the complainant for a written statement of the case, together with a list of his witnesses, and such other information as may have a proper bearing upon the charge. He shall also call upon the accused for such counter-statement as he may wish to make.

685. Officers making either complaints or explanations shall confine themselves exclusively to the facts of the case, and shall neither express an opinion nor impugn the motives of the opposite party.

686. If, after the investigation of a report against an officer, the commanding officer shall not deem the offense one requiring the action of a board of investigation he shall himself take such action as he may deem necessary within the limits of regulation and law.

687. If, upon such investigation, the commanding officer shall be satisfied that the charge is such as to call for the action of the Department, he shall transmit to the Secretary of the Treasury a report embracing the charges and specifications relating to the case. Under such circumstances the accused may be continued under suspension or arrest to await the decision of the Secretary of the Treasury.

688. Should the decision of the Secretary be that no trial take place the accused shall be at once restored to duty. But if it be decided that the accused shall be brought to trial a board of investigation shall be convened for that purpose as soon as the interests of the public service will allow.

689. Whenever an accusation is made against an officer, either by report or indorsement upon a communication, or charges are preferred against him, a copy of such report, indorsement, or charges shall be furnished at the time to the officer accused.

690. An officer is strictly forbidden to criticise or impugn the character, competency, or motives of another officer in any private letter directed to an officer or person connected with the administration of the Treasury Department.

691. On complaint being made against an officer, and in every case requiring immediate decision, a commanding officer may suspend or place in arrest an inferior not longer than ten days, unless a further period is necessary to bring the offender to trial.

692. Officers are not to be suspended for light or trivial offenses, but for such the commanding officer may express his disapprobation, which, in most cases, will answer the purpose of maintaining discipline. An admonition or caution in the ordinary course of duty shall not be considered as a reprimand in the sense of punishment.

693. The captain of a vessel or other competent authority may release temporarily and put on duty an officer under suspension or arrest should an emergency of the service or other sufficient cause make such measure necessary. This temporary release shall not be a bar to any subsequent investigation or trial.

694. When a commanding officer shall suspend, or place in arrest, an officer, he shall call upon the latter for an explanation in writing of the complaint made against him, with a list of persons to be questioned, and shall promptly institute an inquiry into the circumstances in order to regulate his further proceedings. If, after such inquiry, he shall not deem a report to the Department requisite, the officer shall, within ten days, be restored to duty; but when it is a complaint of oppression made by an inferior against a superior officer, and the latter is restored to duty, the commanding officer shall, if it be requested, give in writing his reasons for the restoration to the officer making the complaint, who shall have the right of appeal to higher authority. If the complainant shall decide to appeal the commanding officer shall transmit to the Secretary of the Treasury a full statement of the case, accompanied by the statements of the parties to the controversy.

695. Offenses shall not be allowed to accumulate in order that sufficient matter may thus be collectively obtained for trial, without giving due notice to the offender; and no officer who has been formally reprimanded by the Department for an offense shall be subsequently tried therefor, nor shall the same be subject again to inquiry except when it may be necessary to prove a particular habit charged, or for the due administration of justice.

696. Malicious, vexatious, or frivolous charges against any one will subject the accuser to all the pains and penalties of such conduct.

697. No person in the Revenue Cutter Service shall be tried or punished for any crime or offense connected with the service which shall appear to have been committed more than two years before the issuing of the order for such trial, unless for some manifest impediment he shall not have been amenable to justice within that period.

698. Every officer, when placed in arrest, shall deliver up his sword through the arresting officer to the captain of the vessel. He shall confine himself to the limits assigned him under pain of dismissal from the service. An officer under arrest shall not visit officially his commanding officer, unless sent for; and in case of business requiring attention, he shall make it known in writing.

699. No officer placed under suspension or arrest shall be confined to his room or restrained from the proper use of any part of the vessel except the quarter-deck, bridge, and pilot house, unless such confinement or restraint shall be necessary for the safety of the vessel or the preservation of good order and discipline.

700. No officer who may have been placed in arrest has any right to insist upon being tried by a board, or to persist in considering himself under the restraint of such arrest after he shall have been released, or to refuse to return to the exercise of his duty.

701. Commanding officers shall not impose upon persons under their command any other punishments than the following:

(1) Upon commissioned officers—
   Private reprimand; suspension from duty; arrest or confinement for a period not longer than ten days, except as provided in paragraph 691.

(2) Upon enlisted men (for a single offense or at any one time), either—
   Reduction of any rating established by himself; confinement, with or without irons, single or double, not exceeding ten days; confinement on bread and water not exceeding five days; deprivation of liberty on shore; extra duties.

702. All punishments inflicted by a commanding officer, or by his order, except reprimands, shall be fully entered in the log. This entry must include the rank or rating of the offender, the date and nature of the offense, and the kind and degree of punishment. The termination of the punishment shall be noted also.

703. The commanding officer shall use every endeavor to assure himself that subordinates exercise no cruelty toward persons in confinement, and that the latter suffer no unusual treatment without his knowledge and authority.

704. All reports of misconduct shall be investigated by the commanding officer before punishment is adjudged. After inquiring into the facts in each case and according both accuser and accused an impartial hearing, he shall assign a punishment when necessary. He shall direct the release of every person confined upon the expiration of the term of confinement.

705. An officer having occasion to report an enlisted man for any cause whatever shall make the report to the executive officer.

706. All punishments consisting of extra duties shall be discontinued on Sunday.

707. Care shall be taken not to confine intoxicated men in such a place or manner as may be dangerous in their condition.

708. No commissioned officer shall take part personally in the arrest of a drunken man further than may be absolutely necessary, but the arrest shall always be made by a petty officer or seaman.

709. The commanding officer may restrict or confine a commissioned officer to the limits of the vessel for an offense which, in the former's judgment, merits such punishment; but such restriction or confinement shall not continue longer than ten days.

710. Whenever any person in the Revenue-Cutter Service who shall have been placed under suspension, arrest, or confinement, or otherwise punished for misconduct, shall be released and entirely discharged by competent authority, such discharge shall be a bar to further disciplinary proceedings in the case as far as the interests of the Service are concerned.

Redress of Wrongs.

711. If any person in the Revenue-Cutter Service shall consider himself oppressed by his superior, or observe in him any misconduct, he shall not on that account fail in his respectful bearing toward him, but shall represent such oppression or misconduct, through the official channels, to proper authority. He will be held accountable, however, if his representations be found vexatious, frivolous, or false.

712. An application for a redress of wrong shall be made in writing.

713. When an application for redress of wrong is made to the commanding officer and he shall consider that the alleged wrong is of sufficient gravity to warrant the action of higher authority, he shall submit a report of the case, together with all the correspondence relating thereto, to the Secretary of the Treasury.

714. No officer has the right to demand a board of investigation on himself or others, the granting of a trial resting solely in the discretion of the officer authorized to convene a board.

APPENDIX E.

EXPLANATION OF GENERAL SCOTT WITH REFERENCE TO THE ARMY REGULATIONS OF 1821.

WASHINGTON, *May 2, 1822.*

Major General Scott has the honor to submit to the committee of the House of Representatives, to which was referred a resolution relative to the regulations of the Army, the following "condensed statement of facts," and shall be happy to furnish any further explanation in his power that may be required by the committee.

General Scott compiled all the articles of the book originally submitted to Congress, and many of the others, and was the editor of the whole.

He brought the manuscript of that part of the book submitted to Congress with him to Washington, in December, 1820, and intended to request leave to superintend the printing of it for the use of Congress; but his duties called him away from Washington on the 28th or 29th of the same month. As soon as the book was out of the press of the Public Printer, General Scott received, at Philadelphia, some four or five copies sent to him by request, and from several persons. He immediately perceived that the impression contained many typographical errors; and, on a more attentive examination (which the *printed* form enabled him to make), he discovered that some parts of the book did not perfectly harmonize with each other, and that *principles* laid down in other articles required a fuller development. Fearful that the book would be immediately acted on by Congress, he hastily sent to the chairman of the Military Committee of the House, direct, a copy containing such corrections as first occurred to him, and proceeded somewhat more at his leisure to render the book as perfect as it was in his power to make it. General Scott has now ascertained that it was on the 20th February, 1821, that he sent a copy, with *all* his corrections, through the War Department, to the same committee. This copy was the exact duplicate of another retained by him, both corrected in red ink, and verified in the most particular manner. About the 2d March he received a letter from Gen. A. Smyth, chairman, etc., advising him, General Scott, that the corrected copy had been received, and that the fourteenth section of the act of 2d March, 1821, had been added to a bill from the Senate, by way of amendment, etc. Early in the same month, General Scott received instructions to put the book to the press for the use of the Army. All the proof sheets of the new impression passed under the inspection of General Scott, and he solemnly avers that all the articles which had been before Congress for sanction were strictly reprinted from the corrected duplicate copy retained by General Scott, as above stated, and that the article 75 was one of those which had been previously so corrected. He is confirmed in his strong recollection on this subject by the positive conviction that he received no suggestion from anybody to alter article 75, but was himself induced to insert the words "except in extraordinary cases," at the time the other corrections were made, in order that the rule might correspond with the analogous but stronger case contained in article 4, paragraph 1, where the same words will be found. The latter rule has existed in our service since the year 1813, at least.

General Scott has said, above, that the articles which were first printed for the use of Congress were strictly reprinted, after the duplicate copy retained by him. He ought to have said that they were reprinted in the most perfect good faith, as he recollects to have made, perhaps, two or three *verbal* corrections, after the 20th February, 1821, merely with a view to grammatical propriety; and he also recollects that article 38 ("organization of departments") was slightly altered at the time it was reprinted; as thus: the words "major general of the division" were stricken out, and so was "*assistant*," before the words "inspector general." These changes it was thought were rendered necessary by the act that sanctioned the regulations, and which gave to the Army a *new* organization in those particulars.

The foregoing statement is made on the strength of a memory that has but rarely deceived. General Scott has not had in his hands (in all, *five minutes*,) a copy of the regulations as printed for the use of Congress, in the last ten months.

All of which is most respectfully submitted.

WINFIELD SCOTT,
Major General by brevet.

P. S.—General Scott begs leave to add, that, to the best of his knowledge and belief, not a principle embraced by the work originally laid before Congress has been changed or impaired by the alterations and amendments above noticed.

WINFIELD SCOTT.

APPENDIX F.

LETTER OF SECRETARY OF WAR BELKNAP, ACCOMPANYING PROPOSED REGULATIONS OF 1873.

WAR DEPARTMENT,
Washington City, February 17, 1873.

To the HOUSE OF REPRESENTATIVES OF THE UNITED STATES:

The Secretary of War has the honor to transmit, for the consideration of the House of Representatives, a system of regulations for the administration of the affairs of the Army, prepared in accordance with the provisions of section 20 of the act approved July 15, 1870. Soon after the passage of that act a board of officers was assembled, who, after much labor and inquiry into the practical needs of the service, finally prepared these regulations, which, with some modifications, are submitted. From the detailed nature of the work it was found impossible to prepare it in time to be presented at the third session of the Forty-first Congress, as required by the act.

It is proper, in submitting them, to observe that they are merely regulations in aid or complement to the statutes, and define and prescribe the details for carrying on the routine work of the Army. The act of July 28, 1866, section 37, chapter 299, declares that the existing regulations shall remain in force until Congress shall have acted upon a code of regulations to be prepared by the Secretary of War.

The regulations then and now in force are those of 1863. They are ten years old, and no longer adapted to the condition of Army affairs, but under the act of 1866 it is impossible for the Executive to change them. The length of a letter on a knapsack, for example, being prescribed therein, the Executive has no power to alter its size until Congress shall authorize it, and the regulations now presented will be subject to precisely the same objection, and if they are to be made law, not to be altered or amended save by act of Congress, there are many provisions that it would be wise not to present, as experience may show that alterations may be necessary. The Secretary of War therefore earnestly recommends to Congress that, if formally approved by that body, they be made subject *to such alterations as the President may from time to time adopt.*

WM. W. BELKNAP,
Secretary of War.

APPENDIX G.

REPORT OF COMMITTEE ON MILITARY AFFAIRS, HOUSE OF REPRESENTATIVES.

IN REGARD TO THE

Promulgation of "Revised Army Regulations." (H. R. bill 844), with views of officers, as published in House Report No. 592, 43d Congress, 1st Session.

In the twentieth section of the act approved July 15, 1870, entitled "An act making appropriations for the support of the Army for the year ending June 30, 1871, and for other purposes," it was provided as follows:

"That the Secretary of War shall prepare a system of general regulations for the administration of the affairs of the Army, which, when approved by Congress, shall be in force and obeyed until altered or revoked by the same authority; and the said regulations shall be reported to Congress at its next session: *Provided*, That said regulations shall not be inconsistent with the laws of the United States."

In accordance with the provisions of the law the Secretary of War caused "Revised Army Regulations" to be prepared by a board of officers, and on the 17th of February, 1873, the Secretary of War submitted a copy of said "Revised Army Regulations" to the House of Representatives, accompanied with a note, in which he said:

"Soon after the passage of that act (July 15, 1870), a board of officers was assembled, who, after much labor and inquiry into the practical needs of the service, finally prepared these regulations, which, with some modifications, are submitted. From the detailed nature of the work it was found impossible to prepare it in time to be presented at the third session of the Forty-first Congress, as required by the act."

This report came to the Military Committee of the Forty-second Congress at such a late day of the session that it was impossible for the committee or the Forty-second Congress to act upon it.

The Committee on Military Affairs on the 6th of March, 1873, made the following report:

"That they were referred to them within a few days past; that they are voluminous, and that there is not sufficient time to consider the same, and therefore ask that the same be printed."

Ever since the assembling of the Forty-third Congress the "Revised Army Regulations" have been under consideration, and the Committee on Military Affairs sensibly feel the gravity and importance of the work comprehended in these regulations, but are far from satisfied that they are just the thing in all respects required for the government of the Army, and therefore hesitate to recommend their adoption by Congress, and thereby give them the force and effect of law for the control of the Army and the management of the military affairs of the country. Doubtless many of the provisions are excellent and would be very desirable, while others are open to objection and which in practice would not conduce to the harmonious government of the Army. The committee feel that it would not answer the best purposes of the Army to incorporate the proposed "Revised Army Regulations" into the military system of the country by legal enactment.

The committee feel fortified and confirmed in this conclusion from the opinions which they have elicited from a number of able and experienced Army officers, to whom the proposed regulations were submitted. These officers question the propriety of Congress adopting these regulations, and are of opinion that they would not work to the advantage of the Army. The committee append to this report the statements of these officers upon the subject.

Army regulations should be flexible, so as to allow of their change or modification as circumstances and the exigencies of the public service may require; they ought not, in the opinion of the committee, to be absolute, and which could only be annulled or changed by act of Congress.

The Articles of War should be the fixed law for the government of the Army, and the regulations ought to grow out of these as the limbs do out of a tree; the limbs may be cut off or trimmed, but the tree remains. Articles of War and regulations ought to sustain the same relationship to each other. There ought to be power lodged somewhere outside of Congress to make and change regulations when there is occasion for so doing. The committee therefore report the following bill:

"*Be it enacted, etc.*, That so much of section 20 of the act approved July 15, 1870, entitled 'An act making appropriations for the support of the Army for the year ending June 30, 1871, and for other purposes,' as requires the system of general regulations for the Army therein authorized to be reported to Congress at its next session, and approved by that body, be, and the same is hereby, repealed; and the President is hereby authorized, under said section, to make and publish regulations for the government of the Army in accordance with existing laws."

Views on proposed new Army Regulations, by Maj. Gen. W. S. Hancock, Gen. N. A. Miles, Gen. John Pope, Gen. E. D. Townsend, Gen. R. B. Marcy, Gen. N. H. Davis, Gen. R. S. Roberts, Gen. J. J. Reynolds, and Capt. Kinzie Bates.

NEW YORK CITY, *January 22, 1874.*

GENERAL: In compliance with your recent suggestion, I have made a general examination of the proposed new regulations for the Army, and having observed some features which particularly struck me as objectionable, I give herewith my views thereon as follows:

The Constitution of the United States says: "Congress shall have power to make rules for the government and regulation of the land and naval forces."

The acts of Congress on this subject read as follows:

Act of March 3, 1813: "It shall be the duty of the Secretary of the War Department, and he is hereby authorized, to prepare general regulations," etc., "which regulations, when approved by the President of the United States, shall be respected and obeyed until altered or revoked by the same authority. And the said general regulations, thus prepared and approved, shall be laid before Congress at their next session."

The act of April 24, 1816: "The regulations in force before the reduction of the Army be recognized as far as the same shall be found applicable to the service, subject, however, to such alterations as the Secretary of War may adopt with the approbation of the President."

The act of July 28, 1866: "The Secretary of War be, and he is hereby, directed to have prepared, and to report to Congress at its next session, a code of regulations for the government of the Army, and of the militia in actual service, which shall embrace all necessary orders and forms of a general character, for the performance of all duties incumbent on officers and men in the military service, including rules for the government of courts martial. The existing regulations to remain in force until Congress shall have acted on said report."

The act of July 15, 1870: "The Secretary of War shall prepare a system of general regulations for the administration of the affairs of the Army, which when approved by Congress, shall be in force and obeyed until altered or revoked by the same authority, and said regulations shall be reported to Congress at its next session: *Provided*, That the said regulations shall not be inconsistent with the laws of the United States."

Unless the Articles of War be so considered, Congress does not appear even to have exercised directly its constitutional power to "make rules for the government of the land and naval forces;" but, on the contrary, has placed the labor of preparation on the President and Secretary of War, and reserved to itself only the duty of approving the rules made by these officers.

The Supreme Court of the United States has decided that "the power of the Executive to establish rules and regulations for the government of the Army is undoubted. The power to establish implies necessarily the power to modify, or repeal, or to create anew." And the Attorney General has given the opinion that "the War Department, representing the President in the administration of the Army, has permanent authority from Congress to make regulations in aid and complement of statutes."

The regulations now before Congress for its approval are those submitted in compliance with the act of July 15, 1870, which says that when they are approved by Congress they shall be in force and obeyed until altered or revoked by the same authority. The power which the Supreme Court and Attorney-General find the Executive to possess for establishing regulations and modifying, repealing, and creating them anew, will not, therefore, apply to the proposed code if adopted under this statute. In fact it can not be supposed that it applies to any code adopted by Congress without a special provision of Congress conferring upon the Executive, instead of reserving to itself, the power in question. On the contrary, it must apply only to those "regulations in aid and complement of statutes" to which the Attorney-General refers.

The article of the Constitution which gives Congress power to make rules for the Army would scarcely be regarded if that duty were delegated absolutely and entirely to some one else; and Congress would have to repeal the act of July, 1870, and would place itself in a peculiar attitude if it should confer on the President power to change immediately and entirely a code of regulations which had just received Congressional sanction as right and wise.

The foregoing leads to the conclusion that to conform exactly to the Constitution the "general regulations" called for by the act of July, 1870, should be adopted by Congress as the Articles of War now in force were, and that as prescribed in said act they should not be altered or revoked, except by authority of Congress.

Furthermore, consideration for the good of the service leads to the same conclusion. There are certain general rules concerning organization, rank, command, appointments, promotions, rewards, punishments, discipline (including military courts), compliments, responsibility for public money and property, etc., which should be established by Congress, known to the service as so established, and changeable only by Congress. This, it seems to me, is necessary to put into the military service an element of certainty and stability required for its good management.

But in addition to these rules, in aid and complement of them, issued and administered with them, should come that large mass of regulations, in detail, which the Supreme Court finds the President has undoubted right to make and modify at his pleasure, and which we all know it is necessary he should so make and modify.

The code now before Congress, excellent in many respects, is objectionable on account of embracing altogether too much for congressional approval or sanction. There are some things in military affairs which are above, and others which are beneath congressional action. This code contains both. As an example of the former it is enough to state that it prescribes the manner of conducting marches, sieges, defenses, of fighting battles, etc. That is to say, it establishes rules to which the science of war must conform. It would be as well to enact rules to govern the science of astronomy.

The parts of the proposed code here referred to fail to exhibit that consistency with the laws of the United States which is required by the act of July, 1870, in response to which the code is submitted. They are in fact essays setting forth the views of the writers upon various unsettled military subjects, to which it is manifestly unnecessary that congressional sanction should be given. The effect produced by congressional indorsement of these views may be somewhat mitigated by delegating to the President authority to undo the action of Congress, but it is certainly far better not to so involve the subject.

Those things which are beneath congressional action form a large part of the code, appearing in the details laid down for the interior management of bureaus, arms of service, regiments, companies, etc.; such, for example, as the following, taken at random, in which Congress is asked to enact that "whenever a patient is transferred from the care of one medical officer to another, the account of his case, taken from the record, shall accompany him;" that "paymasters while making payments to troops shall be in uniform;" that "immediately after a man has enlisted the recruiting officer will have his hair cut close," that "during warm weather the ice shall be distributed under the direction of the post commander;" that "the noncommissioned officer in charge of the mess-room will see that no soldier goes to the mess-table unless perfectly clean and in uniform;" that "captains will require their lieutenants to assist them in the performance of all company duties;" that "on the plains, when forage can not be obtained, grazing should be allowed at every spare moment, and as long as possible, especially early in the morning when the dew is on the grass;" that, "when practicable, bran mash is to be given once a week; never oftener than twice a week, except to purge;" that "a horse's feet should be stripped with clay or cow manure at least once a week;" and that "the sheath must be washed once a week with castile soap, and then greased."

The wisdom of these rules is not under discussion. The point made is that they do not require the action of Congress and had better be left with the Executive. Furthermore, the code, beside being defective in giving detailed regulations to Congress, under a resolution which called for general regulations for the government of our service, fails to be fully responsive to the resolution in being to a large extent inapplicable to our Army. This is a grave defect. One serious difficulty encountered by those who administer, as well as those who obey, our Army regulations is the great number and bulk of them. It is, therefore, a primary consideration that they shall contain nothing but what is necessary. They are made "for the administration of the affairs of the Army," and every one of them should be applicable to the affairs of our Army as we are now conducting them, or to its affairs as we are likely to conduct them in case of hostilities. This will not admit of our enlarging the regulations and bewildering those concerned with them by embodying in the code a great mass of rules and theories which have no application whatever to any part of our military organization as established by existing laws; much less will it admit of the introduction of rules for organizations that we have never had, or that we have tried and abandoned. There are many rules in the proposed code coming under these heads; some of them read as if they had been translated *verbatim* from foreign services. That part of article 1 headed "staff," hereafter quoted, is a sample of this. Another may be found on page 3, reading thus: "The regiment is not, as such, a tactical unit. It is an organization composed of * * * from eight to sixteen batteries, including those at the depot." We have no regiment of artillery of either eight or sixteen batteries (our regiments containing just twelve). We have no depots for part of the batteries of a regiment, and never had. The nearest approach to this form of organization we ever made was in 1861, when we created some new regiments of infantry, composed each of three battalions, and for a time indulged in the theory that one of them would be a depot battalion; but we were disappointed in the practical working of this organization, and subsequently abolished it by law. Then why now encumber the regulations made for our daily guidance with a likeness of it assumed for the artillery. Many other examples could be given.

But besides the foregoing objections to the general plan of the code, there are objections to certain important particulars in it. It is only practicable here to refer to some of them.

On page 10 there is a regulation saying that "in each grade officers will take precedence by date of commission or appointment, excepting that whenever military operations may require the presence of two or more officers of the same grade in the same field or department, the President may assign the command of the forces to any officer of the highest grade present, without reference to date of commission."

The authority given to the President by the last part of this regulation, to make an exceptional assignment, is directly inconsistent with existing laws. The power to make such exceptional assignment was conferred on the President by special act of Congress during the late war, but it was repealed by the act of July, 1866.

On page 11 it is stated, "commands are exercised by virtue of office or by special assignment of officers having military rank, and who are eligible by law to such commands."

The meaning of this paragraph is not plain. The principle it should enunciate is that office and rank in the Army are conferred by the President and Senate, that they render the officer eligible to command, but that he exercises command by virtue of assignment and not "by virtue of office."

Page 104. Article LV. is headed "Staff." "The staff is divided into—

"1st. The general staff, composed of the generals of the Army who command troops, and the officers who aid them in the direction of military operations.

"2d. The administration services."

If this paragraph is not inconsistent with any existing statute, it *is* inconsistent with our military history, the character of our military establishment, and with a long established custom of our service; (this custom, if not statute law, is generally good law). It is inconsistent with the definition on page 3, where the theory of the military establishment is given. There we are told that "the staff includes all officers who aid general officers in the performance of their duties, and those who provide the needful supplies and minister to the various wants of the Army. It consists of a general staff and of special staffs, or administrative services.

"The general staff includes the chief of staff, the officers of the Adjutant-General's and Inspector-General's Departments, and all officers acting in these capacities," etc.

The effect of the paragraph under discussion is, by an obscure definition, to lay the foundation for changing the status of the general officers of the Army. Under our theory and late practice, they have been simply general officers—that is, officers eligible to the command of all arms and branches of the service and exercising that command by virtue of assignment under the rank held by them from the Government, and not by virtue of being the staff officers of some higher functionary by whose delegated authority they act. To call them staff officers is an unwise imitation of certain foreign systems—the French, notably—in which all general officers are regarded as on the staff of the sovereign, from whom, in point of fact, they derive their authority.

These remarks apply to the General, Lieutenant General, major generals, and brigadier generals in our service who were appointed to those offices for the purpose of acting as commanders, and not to brigadier generals at the head of certain staff, corps, and departments, who were appointed thereto as staff officers and for staff duties.

The manner of appointment in these two classes is of itself evidence that the members of the latter class do, and those of the former do not belong to the staff.

Again, without discussing the technical meaning of the word "staff," it is safe to say that with us a staff officer does not, as such, command, but that he is necessarily an officer whose duty it is, directly or indirectly, to aid some commander in carrying out his, the commander's, views. In this light the general officers of our Army do not belong in the paragraph of the proposed code quoted above, and headed "Staff."

On page 1, under the head of "Theory of the military establishment," we are told that "the Army is composed of the troops and the staff." This, in a foreign language, may be a correct definition for some foreign army, but in English it does not convey a correct idea; certainly not to us, in relation to our Army. The word "troops" is immediately afterward defined as meaning "organized corps or bodies of combatants." This is giving an undue restriction to the meaning of "troops." It is a word in such common use that its accepted signification should not be changed in regulations; certainly not unless to gain some greater good than has yet appeared. We say the British troops, the rebel troops, the white troops, the regular troops, the volunteer troops. We tell a commander to bring up his troops, march off his troops, etc., never limiting the meaning of the word to "organized corps or bodies of combatants," and excluding the staff, etc. The word "line" should be defined as used in phrase "details in the line," page 4. Is it equivalent in meaning to "troops?"

On page 15 it is set forth that "no officer shall be commissioned on the staff who has not, for at least one year just previous, been on duty with troops." The meaning of this rule is doubtful. Is it the intention that officers now in the staff shall not, when promoted to a higher grade, be commissioned unless they have been "on duty with troops at least one year just previous," or is the restriction to apply only to officers when first appointed to the staff? Again, what is meant by "on duty with troops?" Is the commanding general of an army, an expedition, or a military department "on duty with troops?" If so, is not his staff on duty in like manner; or is the character of an officer's service in the case under consideration to be decided solely by considering his station—his place of abode—for the time being?

Whatever the correct answers to these questions may be, it seems clear that this regulation imposes, to say the least of it, an unnecessary limitation on the appointing power. The best qualified and most deserving should be selected to be commissioned in the staff, and it would be wrong to the service and to the individual to exclude any such for not having "been on company or regimental duty at least one year just previous."

When officers likely to be commissioned in the staff are not with their companies, it is because they are properly absent for reasons satisfactory to the authority competent to decide such matters, and usually in the performance of duties which especially fit them for positions in the staff.

The object of the regulation is, doubtless, to coerce officers into remaining with their companies, and thus contribute to obtaining, by a kind of indirection, an object which the Secretary of War and General in Chief can always secure by direct action, if they deem it desirable. This regulation is similar in its general character and object to that which immediately follows it, saying that "colonels of regiments and captains of companies will not be placed on any duty (except general courts-martial and courts of inquiry) which shall separate them from their commands, without the special order of the President," etc.

It is a fact within the experience of all of us, colonels and captains are needed with their regiments and companies, and it is for this reason the law authorizes them, and generally they are with their proper commands; but it is nevertheless a fact that there are exceptional instances when these officers can render more valuable service on detached duty. The President can not look into these details, and the power should be left with those who actually control the Army to place all subordinates where they will do the most good. Whether that is with a regiment or company, with a general officer or a board to make regulations for the Army or the like, can be better decided in each case by commanders, as it comes up with the facts, than by a general rule made in the regulations to meet the case before it arises. General regulations to cover exceptional cases usually do more harm than good.

For consistency the paragraph regarding the absence of captains should be made to agree with the one on page 36. There it is stated that captains "are subject to the temporary details of service as far as courts-martial, military boards," etc. "Military boards," etc., may be construed to authorize absence for a variety of purposes; whereas, the paragraph on page 15 forbids the absence of captains of companies for any duty except "general courts-martial and courts of inquiry."

On page 4 it is stated "The command of a division or department will embrace all the regular forces stationed within it, as well as such volunteer and militia as may be called into the service of the General Government to aid in its defense."

This general rule is immediately followed by a long list of exceptions in these terms: "The Military Academy, engineer troops, general depots of supplies, all arsenals, permanent forts in process of construction or extensive repairs, general recruiting depots, and officers employed on duty not military, are excepted from the operation of the foregoing paragraph, at the discretion of the Secretary of War."

The rule and the exceptions nearly neutralize each other. In fact, the only rule which can be safely announced on this point is the general one hereinbefore enunciated, to the effect that officers command according to their assignment. The order making an original assignment should set forth what it embraces. Commanders succeeding the first one exercise authority to the same extent their predecessors did, unless otherwise ordered.

The sixty-second article of war provides about all the exceptions that should be made to the foregoing principle of assignment. It says: "If, upon marches, guards, or in quarters, different corps of the Army should happen to join or do duty together, the officer highest in rank of the line of the Army, Marine Corps, or militia, by commission, there on duty or in quarters, shall command the whole, and give orders for what is needful to the service, unless otherwise specially directed by the President of the United States, according to the nature of the case."

The next paragraph on this page (4) defines the authority of division commanders thus: "The commander of a geographical division exercises a supervision over the affairs of the departments under his control similar to that which a general commanding an army in the field would exercise over his subordinate commanders, without necessarily interfering with the administration of the commanders."

This is too indefinite for regulations. The division commander may be not sufficiently familiar with the "control which a general commanding an army in the field would exercise," to make this regulation any guide to him. The last part of the regulation telling the division commander not to interfere unnecessarily with the administration of his department commanders is hardly needed, as he is quite certain to think it necessary before he interferes.

On page 16 rules governing leaves of absence to officers are given. Post commanders may grant seven days, department commanders thirty days, and division commanders sixty days (including any leave granted by department commanders). Then it is stated that "all applications for a leave of absence for a time exceeding four months will be submitted through the proper channels to the Secretary of War for approval."

The code, probably through oversight, does not give anyone authority to grant leave for a period between sixty days and four months, and does not give the General of the Army authority to grant any leave at all.

On page 167, under the head of "Transfer of supplies," it is stated:

"The Subsistence Department will be responsible for and have control over the transportation of its supplies. Purchasing and depot commissaries will arrange for all transportation of their supplies whenever rail or water transportation can be contracted for or hired.

"Where supplies are to be transported to posts away from rail or water, the commissary will make requisition upon the depot quartermaster at the place or point where such supplies leave rail or water, for the Government wagons, etc., necessary for their transportation to their destination. If the quartermaster can not furnish such Government transportation, the commissary will hire wagons or contract for the delivery of the supplies at the place of destination. At points of transhipment where there are no suitable public buildings, the commissary will hire or build such storehouses as may be necessary to preserve the supplies."

There is no proof that defects in the present system of transferring supplies render a change of that system necessary, nor that the change proposed would remedy the defects if they existed. The only argument that I know of put forward in support of this change is that the officers of the Subsistence Department giving general satisfaction in the purchase of provisions, they would, if made also responsible for their delivery, be more successful in providing transportation and store-room for what they purchase than the officers of the Quartermaster's Department are. This conclusion is quite unwarranted. The duty of purchasing provisions, and the duty of getting them to their destination, are entirely different. The power of pleasing is embraced in the very nature of the former, while that of disappointing and displeasing is almost inseparable from the latter. The transaction between buyer and seller, especially where the former has cash to pay, is a very simple one, resting with two individuals and closed up at once. Transporting the thing bought is by no means simple; it involves arrangements, contract, etc., with individuals, railroads, ships, steamboats, wagons, and the like, which in their execution occupy a long time, and this service can not be constantly under the control or even the eye of the Government officers responsible for its execution.

These inherent differences can not be removed or affected by transferring the transportation service from the Quartermaster's Department to the Subsistence Department. The good of the service, so far as it depends on systems, will certainly be more apt to be secured by having the transportation for the whole Army done by the Quartermaster's Department, as now, and pursued therein as a specialty, which its importance demands, than by the change proposed.

I raise no question here as to whether the purchasing of supplies could be done by the Quartermaster's Department. What I mean to assert is, my opinion that the transportation service for the entire army should be conducted by the Quartermaster's Department.

This regulation has the special objection of not stating positively whether wagon transportation for subsistence stores shall be furnished by the Quartermaster or Subsistence Department. The latter must provide the railroad and water transportation; but when it wants wagon transportation, it must first apply for it to the Quartermaster's Department; if this application fails, it then gets its own wagons, etc. Here doubt, confusion, and delay will inevitably arise. Besides, the chiefs of these two Bureaus will never know how much transportation each may have to furnish during the year, and will not be able to make understandingly estimates for transportation appropriations.

Without going further into the subject, I venture the prediction that the proposed regulation would in time of peace result in confusion and unnecessary expense, and in time of war in greater mischief.

(Pages 67, 68, and 69.) It is thought to be hostile to the best interests of the service that artillery and engineer forces when assigned to Army corps and divisions should be on the footing of troops "attached" for service merely, or that they should under such circumstances form special and to a degree independent commands under officers of their own corps or arm of service.

The paragraph referred to, page 68, evidently contemplates officers commanding engineers or artillery forces serving with corps or divisions shall be, in a measure, independent of corps and division commanders (this may certainly be inferred from that portion of the paragraph which provides for their appointing general courts martial, etc.), thus giving the engineers and artillery superior authority in matters of courts martial and otherwise (within the corps or division), to the commanders of those bodies. This would place the corps or division commanders in subordinate positions to the artillery and engineer commanders of the same Army, regardless of what their relative rank might be. It is thought to be common sense and much safer that those commanders who fight the troops in time of war, and are responsible for the success or failure of the operations, should have the same control of those special arms as they have over the other arms not designated as special, rather than to have them subject to the commands of officers who would not be responsible whether the battle was lost or won. Such a regulation, when brought to the test of practical operation in the presence of an enemy, would undoubtedly lead to confusion and failure.

It is believed that the effect of paragraph 9, page 69, would be mischievous and subversive of discipline. It directs officers o. engineers and artillery to make reports of "their operations in all that concerns their specialties" to the headquarters of their respective arms, and this when they may be serving immediately under the orders of corps or division commanders, and notwithstanding they are required to make a report of their operations to their corps or other immediate commander, which he might or might not approve in detail, a copy of which is to be sent to the headquarters of their special arms (without even waiting for the corps commander's remarks or approval); they are here invited to give their own versions of the same operations in a special report, a copy of which is not required to be sent to the corps commander, and which is not even directed to be transmitted through him, thus in a very peculiar way, calling for separate reports of the same operations, which may differ, and one of which is concealed from the view of the corps commander.

In regard to the service of artillery in times of active operations, it is believed that the most practicable and efficient system is that of assigning batteries (from the reserve artillery of the

Army) to the different Army corps, and placing at the corps headquarters an officer of that arm who shall perform the duties of chief or commander of the artillery of the corps under the orders of the corps commander. This was the system pursued in the Army of the Potomac in the latter part of our late war, and was found to answer well its purpose when strictly carried out and not interfered with by the chief of that arm at superior headquarters, who may or not be on the ground, and who may be disposed to have the artillery used according to his own views, although he has no responsibility (as the commander of the troops has) to make his judgment careful. As an instance in point, when this system was interfered with, I may state here that at "Gettysburgh," during the last day of the battle, when I commanded the left center of our army, composed of three corps, there was a portion of my line on which there was no infantry, and while the enemy's great cannonade was in progress, just previous to their grand assault, I rode to that point and found that the guns of a battery posted there were silent, although other batteries on the line were firing slowly. I sent orders by my chief of artillery to the commander of the battery (which happened to belong to the reserve artillery of the Army, and had been sent up to strengthen that part of the line during the assault then impending), to open fire at once, so that it would appear to the enemy that that point was strongly defended, it being very undesirable on account of there being no infantry there that the enemy should select that point for their attack. This order was not obeyed, and I was informed that the battery commander had orders not to fire, from the chief of artillery of the Army of the Potomac. I then rode to the battery myself, and was actually compelled to threaten force on my own line of battle before I could cause the battery to fire upon the enemy. I would have been held responsible in the event of the loss of the line, while the chief of artillery of the Army would have had no responsibility in that event.

The length of this communication precludes reference to other points in these regulations which strike me as defective.

Respectfully submitted.

                              WINF'D S. HANCOCK,
                                Major General, U. S. A.

Gen. W. T. SHERMAN,
   United States Army, Washington, D. C.

WAR DEPARTMENT,
Washington City, January 22, 1874.

SIR: I have the honor to inclose for your consideration, in connection with the new Army Regulations, copy of a letter dated December 30, 1873, from Col. N. A. Miles, Fifth Infantry, presenting objections to that part of the regulations which restricts the tenure of office of regimental staff officers to two years' continuous service, with indorsements thereon of the Adjutant General and Inspector General of the Army.

Very respectfully, your obedient servant,
WILLIAM W. BELKNAP,
Secretary of War.

Hon. JOHN COBURN,
Chairman Committee on Military Affairs,
House of Representatives.

HEADQUARTERS FIFTH UNITED STATES INFANTRY,
Fort Leavenworth, Kans., December 30, 1873.

SIR: In the new Army Regulations printed for the use of members of Congress, and to be acted upon during the present session, appears the following paragraph:

"No officer will be appointed adjutant or regimental quartermaster, who has not served at least one year immediately preceding such appointment with his company, and no officer shall hold a staff appointment in his regiment for a longer period than two years at any one time."

To the adoption of this paragraph I have the honor to urge the following, as I conceive, cogent objections.

In the first place, from the standpoint of a regimental commander: The status of the regimental staff, with reference to the regimental commander, is very closely analogous to that of the personal staff of general officers with reference to the general, and upon this latter selection, and on the duration of such detail, no other restriction is in fact imposed than that of the rank of the officers selected. A regimental commander in selecting his staff desires of course to secure competent, well-informed officers of undoubted probity; but beyond this, and a matter scarcely second to it, he desires that his staff should be so thoroughly honorable, congenial, and in sympathy with him, that the most intimate official and personal relations may subsist between them, and that his ideas and plans may be cordially seconded and carried out by them. Only a slight acquaintance with men is necessary to prove that the first class of qualities frequently exist without the latter.

Under existing orders a commanding officer is made, conjointly with his staff, responsible for the public property for which the staff officer makes returns. Such responsibility should not exist without the corresponding liberty to select the subordinates, in whose honor and probity he has confidence, to be intrusted with the custody, transfer, and expenditure of the property in question. If, then, a regimental commander should find those who, in his estimation, combine in a good degree these essential qualities, why should he be deprived of their services immediately upon becoming thoroughly acquainted with them?

If the system of rotation or transfer of officers from staff to line duties is adduced in support of the proposed change, I would respectfully invite attention to the fact that without such change and under the present system that desirable result is secured in the case of regimental staff officers alone of the entire Army. For, before receiving an appointment as regimental adjutant or quartermaster, a subaltern must serve long enough with his regiment to prove his capacity and general worthy character, and this time usually includes his entire service as second lieutenant, and a part of his service as first lieutenant, at least five years in all as an average. Having been appointed a regimental staff officer, he can only hold that position while a subaltern, and, of necessity, returns to duty in the line immediately upon promotion to a captaincy; thus, as I have said, experiencing the supposed desirable alternation of line and staff duties. If the change from staff to line duties is considered advisable, why should not this principle be equally applicable to the general staff of the Army?

From the standpoint of a regimental staff officer I would urge that frequent changes, involving changes of station and of relations with officers, would necessitate great expense; that large property accountability is incurred, and, in the settlement of accounts, much difficulty results if frequent changes are required; that at least half of the two years permitted would be required to become thoroughly accustomed to new duties; and that (inasmuch as each new permanent regimental commander generally makes a new selection of staff officers) from death, resignation, retirement, or permanent detachment of regimental commanders, the tenure of office of a regimental staff officer is now very precarious, and instances are rare in which some one of these casualties does not return such officer to line duty long before he receives the captaincy which, as before stated, necessarily terminates his staff position.

The regimental commanders, with the aid of their staffs, administer the affairs of the regiments, that is of the entire line of the Army. Inasmuch as the proposed change would affect disadvantageously the administration of affairs by these officers, it follows that the Army would not be benefited but injured by it, and I most urgently request that these objections may be referred to the Military Committees in the Houses of Congress, to be duly weighed before the new regulations are adopted.

I have the honor to be, very respectfully, your obedient servant,

       NELSON A. MILES,
    Colonel Fifth United States Infantry.
        Bvt. Maj. Gen. U. S. A.

The Hon. SECRETARY OF WAR,
 Washington, D. C.

[Indorsements.]

HEADQUARTERS DEPARTMENT OF THE MISSOURI,
 Fort Leavenworth, Kans., January 3, 1874.

Respectfully forwarded to the assistant adjutant general, headquarters Military Division of the Missouri.

The general views of Colonel Miles, Fifth Infantry, on the within subject, are fully concurred in by the department commander.

        JOHN POPE,
    Bvt. Maj. Gen. U. S. A., Commanding.

ADJUTANT GENERAL'S OFFICE, *January 12, 1874.*

Respectfully submitted to the Secretary of War. There is much force in Colonel Miles's objections to the regulations referred to. There may be a few cases where colonels will not make the best selections, but they will be very few compared to those where unsuitable officers would be placed in regimental staff positions by detail.

       E. D. TOWNSEND,
       Adjutant General.

WAR DEPARTMENT.
Inspector General's Office, January 21, 1874.

Respectfully returned to the Secretary of War.

The paragraph herein alluded to, was introduced by the board for the reason that regimental staff duties are generally regarded as more desirable than service with companies; and as there are generally several subalterns in every regiment competent to fill those positions, they would endeavor to qualify themselves for the performance of staff duties if the regulation was adopted.

In this way a much larger number of officers would be educated in staff duties than under the existing system, and would be available for organizing large armies in time of war, or for promotion in staff corps or departments.

I see no objection to this paper being referred to the Military Committee of the House of Representatives, as Colonel Miles desires.

R. B. MARCY.
Inspector General U. S. A.

FORT MCPHERSON, NEBR., *October 20, 1873.*

MY DEAR GENERAL: The copy of proposed Regulations for the Army, including revised Rules and Articles of War, was duly received. I have glanced over them with considerable care, and hope they will be adopted by Congress. The suggestion of the Secretary of War should, by all means, be included, viz, "subject to such alterations as the President may from time to time adopt."

There is one point to which I would invite special attention (if I am not acting officiously in so doing). The Articles of War and Regulations should be very slightly modified so as to conform to General Order No. 5, Headquarters Army, Washington, D. C., June 20, 1873. This order was issued, after the new regulations had been reported, for good and sufficient reasons; it is in strict accordance with the spirit of existing laws, and produces uniformity and harmony in the service.

The only change required would be simply to add to the paragraph preceding the Rules and Articles as now numbered, page 204, these words: "And the term 'company' shall embrace the minimum unit for administration in all arms;" and omit the words "troop and battery" from articles 13, 35, 38, 39, 44, 45, 50, 72, 74, and 84; and direct that in printing the Regulations the Articles of War shall be adhered to. This will require but few and very slight changes.

I can not enter more into detail without troubling you with a long letter. Would like very much to have two hours' interview with the Military Committee before action is taken on these regulations, but that is not in my power. As a whole they are excellent, and by far the best system we have ever had.

I am, General, very truly yours,

J. J. REYNOLDS.

Hon. JOHN COBURN,
   Indianapolis, Indiana.

WAR DEPARTMENT,
Washington City, February 2, 1874.

SIR: I have the honor to inclose for your consideration, in connection with the new Regulations for the Army, copy of a letter of the 10th ultimo from Captain Kinzie Bates, First Infantry, suggesting the appointment of councils of administration, composed of enlisted men, to audit the accounts of "company funds," with opinion, indorsed thereon, of Maj. Gen. W. S. Hancock, commanding Military Division of the Atlantic.

Very respectfully, your obedient servant,

WM. W. BELKNAP,
Secretary of War.

Hon. JOHN COBURN,
   Chairman Committee on Military Affairs,
      House of Representatives.

FORT BRADY, MICHIGAN, *January 10, 1874.*

SIR: The suggestion of General Ord, that where enlisted men are tried by courts-martial, that some of their peers be detailed to sit on their courts, has re-awakened an idea of mine in regard to the company fund. I do not for a moment imagine that the following plan is original with me, but as I have never seen any mention of it. I simply forward it in the hope that it may be worthy the attention of the Commanding General. Numerous complaints are made in the Army and Navy Journal in regard to the expenditure of the company fund. I believe these complaints can be done away with by a company council of administration to consist of three enlisted men, one of whom should be a noncommissioned officer, who should audit the accounts. The proceedings to be approved by an officer's council, consisting of the captain and subalterns of the company. In case of a disapproval of the enlisted men's council by the officers, the matter to be referred to the colonel of the regiment for his decision.

I remain, sir, very respectfully, yours, etc.,

KINZIE BATES,
Captain First Infantry, Commanding Post.

ASSISTANT ADJUTANT GENERAL,
Military Division of the Atlantic.

[Indorsement.]

HEADQUARTERS DIVISION OF THE ATLANTIC,
New York, January 24, 1874.

Respectfully forwarded to the assistant adjutant-general, headquarters of the Army.

I regard the suggestion made within as worthy of consideration in connection with the adoption of a new code of regulations. I understand that the messing expenditures of squads in the British service, though supervised by their officers, are controlled by the men themselves on a plan similar to the one proposed for the company fund, and that it works admirably.

That part of the regulations in regard to company funds, now before Congress, authorizes an *inspection* of the said fund by the enlisted men. The object of the new regulations in this particular would, I think, more probably be obtained by some such systematic plan as that herein suggested, than by the indefinite one in the proposed regulations. (See page 45 of Code now before Congress, or House Doc. 85 of Forty-second Congress, third session.) I do not, however, commit myself to General Ord's suggestion as to detailing enlisted men on courts-martial.

WINF'D S. HANCOCK,
Major General Commanding.

INSPECTOR GENERAL'S DEPARTMENT,
New York City, February 4, 1874.

GENERAL: I have the honor to submit the following in response to the request of your committee, with regard to the code of Army Regulations recently prepared by a board of officers and submitted to Congress for its action thereon.

The following mentioned changes are respectfully suggested, with reasons therefor:

(Page 2.) In first line, last paragraph, insert before "infantry," the word "cavalry," and in the second line omit, "in the cavalry the troop."

Reason: To accord with War Department orders.

(Page 5.) Add to paragraph four, "and the Secretary of War may authorize the enlistment of general service men for the inspectors general."

Reason: Because no clerks are furnished inspectors general, who have important and responsible duties to perform requiring clerical aid.

(Page 15.) Omit paragraph three under Article XII.

Reason: This paragraph would prohibit in some cases the appointment of worthy and suitable officers who may have been ordered on duty, not with troops.

(Page 15.) Next paragraph, omit first two and third lines to include "President," and then read, "Colonels will not be absent from their commands longer than two years," etc.

Reason: Because the paragraph as it stands would often prevent details demanded by the good of the service.

(Page 16.) Under Article XIV, after paragraph five, add this paragraph: "The General in Chief may grant leaves of absence for a period of four months."

Reason: Authority for the General in Chief to grant leaves of absence, seems to have been omitted.

(Page 18.) Under Article XVI, in first line of fourth paragraph, substitute for "censure," "admonition."

Reason: "Censure" implies punishment, which should only be inflicted after a legal hearing, conviction, etc.

(Page 22.) Under Article XXI, first paragraph, change to read, "the commander of a post may give furloughs to soldiers of his command as he shall judge," etc.

Reason: The companies of a regiment are generally stationed at several posts, and sometimes in different districts and departments, over which the regimental commander has no control.

(Page 35.) In last line of fourth paragraph, read "three years" for "two years."

Reason: This period I think better.

(Page 35.) In the second line of the next paragraph, read "six months" for "three months."

Reason: Same as above.

(Page 38.) To the last paragraph add, "and bedding."

Reason: An important matter, affecting health and personal cleanliness.

(Page 39.) In the first paragraph, second line, after the first "the" add "quarters."

Reason: Probably unintentionally omitted.

(Page 44.) In the second line, fifth paragraph, substitute "thirty-three and one-third per cent." for "fifty per cent."

Reason: This saving comes from the soldier's ration, and should be so used as to contribute the most to his benefit, which will be the case by giving the larger portion to the "post fund," there being usually few companies at regimental headquarters. This change accords with the views of officers generally, as expressed to me.

(Page 53.) Under Article XL, fourth paragraph, in first line, add after "morning" "the company quarters, messes, and kitchens, daily."

Reason: A very necessary and important duty.

(Page 100.) In last line of last paragraph, change to read after "will be," "covered into the United States Treasury."

Reason: Required by act of Congress.

The eighty-eighth article of war should be changed, extending the limitation of time within which a person may be brought to trial.

Reason: For the interests of the service.

REMARKS.—The above-suggested alterations are what appear to me proper, from the limited time I have had to examine the subject, in addition to those made in the War Department copy, which have been marked in the copy received from you.

I think it advisable not to make the code of regulations under consideration law, but leave them subject to revision and change by the President of the United States.

A reason for this is, that it is difficult or impossible to make regulations perfect and such as will properly meet all the exigencies of the military service arising under the vicissitudes affecting it; therefore there should be authority in the President to make changes that experience and circumstances seem to demand.

The old edition of Army Regulations, of 1863, is exhausted, many officers being without a copy, and in consequence of many changes therein having been made by acts of Congress, and orders, the Army is much in need of a new code at this time.

The Articles of War should be made law; they are the statutes for the Army, to protect the constitutional rights of officers and enlisted men, and others connected therewith, to insure justice, punish offenses, govern the disbursement of public moneys, provide for the administration of the military branch of the public service, and promote its efficiency, etc.

I think they need revision and changing in some respects.

A penal code of punishment, graduated to the character and magnitude of offenses, should be established for the guide of courts-martial, the better to insure even justice.

This report has been delayed somewhat from unavoidable causes.

I am, General, very respectfully, your obedient servant,

N. H. DAVIS,
Inspector General, U. S. A.

The Hon. CHAIRMAN OF THE MILITARY COMMITTEE,
House of Representatives, Washington, D. C.

Gen. JOHN COBURN,
Chairman of Military Committee,
House of Representatives.

SIR: In compliance with your request, I have the honor to submit, in writing, my views of the new Army Regulations, and the emendations that, in my judgment, should be made before their final adoption by Congress, "as the rules for the government of the Army."

The old Rules and Articles of War adopted by act of Congress approved April 10, 1806, borrowed mainly from England's military act, have been very greatly improved and simplified by elimination of parts inapplicable to our military system, and so otherwise changed as to constitute a very complete code for the administration of justice and enforcement of discipline in the Army.

As a whole system of regulations intended to carry into practical effect the laws of Congress, they are a very great improvement on any previous compilation; and it is with hesitation I have suggested the few changes herein inclosed. My object has been to so change a few of the primary regulations that have controlling authorization over all others, as to avoid conflict of military authority and fix more definitely the purview of the officers of the General Commanding the Army and the Secretary of War; the General being in my view strictly military and executive, and the Secretary civil and administrative.

When the boundaries of these two officers are authoritatively established, and the political patronage of the great contract and supplying departments is severed from the military, fixing the command, government, and discipline of every military arm in the General, the vicious influences that go to weaken discipline and the effectiveness of arms will, in my judgment, be forever avoided.

I am, very respectfully, your obedient servant,
B. S. ROBERTS,
Brevet Brigadier General U. S. A. (retired).

NEW ARMY REGULATIONS.

First. As to the recommendation in the letter of the Secretary of War transmitting to Congress the new regulations for the Army, with revised and corrected Articles of War, that if these regulations are formally approved by Congress, "they be made subject to such alterations as the President may from time to time adopt," I will say that if Congress gives such discretionary power to the President, it will confer on him and his legal representive, the Secretary of War, authority over the Army the Congress can not under the Constitution delegate.

The Constitution (section 8, Article I), in seventeen paragraphs, fixes certain sovereign legislative powers in Congress that are not transferable to the Executive or any Department of the Government. And the thirteenth paragraph is in these words: "The Congress shall have power to make rules for the government and regulation of the land and naval forces."

The powers in this section of the Constitution take the characterization of sovereignty, are forbidden to the States in section 10, and are exclusively and unalterably fixed in Congress. Congress can, therefore, with the same propriety authorize the President or his military representative, the Secretary of War, "from time to time to declare war or to coin money," as "to alter, from time to time, the regulations made by Congress for the government of the Army."

Second. Strike out on page 3, paragraph relating to the engineers, the word "civil," and substitute for it the word "mixed;" because by law of Congress officers of the Army can not discharge civil offices without vacating their military commissions, and, besides, mixed better characterizes the work assigned to an officer of the Army than the word civil.

Third. Strike out the words "regular constitutional" in first line of Article II defining the office of Secretary of War, and substitute for them the word "lawful." The office of Secretary of War is not an office created by the Constitution, but by a law of Congress, approved August 7, 1789. He cannot therefore be said to be "the regular constitutional organ of the President," but he is the lawful organ. For the same reason strike out the words "and constitutional" in the fourth line.

Fourth. It is clear to my mind that Article III requires emendation and a more definite declaration of the scope of the military function of the Commander in Chief of the Army.

The Constitution, that makes the President the Commander in Chief of the Army and Navy, never contemplated giving to him the personal administration or personal supervision of the Army, whether in the field in time of war, or in its garrisons in time of peace. His office under our form of government is mainly civil and by far transcends in its magnitude the military administration of the Army under the laws of Congress. It was clearly the intention of the framers of the Constitution to vest in Congress the control of the Army. And this intention is unequivocally declared in the thirteenth paragraph of section 8 of the Constitution, in the words "the Congress shall have power to make rules for the government and regulation of the land and naval forces."

Add to this his constitutional obligation imposed by section 3, Article II, "he shall take care that the laws be faithfully executed," and the logical legal deduction is plain, that his powers as Commander in Chief of the Army and Navy of the United States, as conferred in section 2, Article II, Constitution, are subordinate to Congress, and limited at its discretion.

The framers of the Constitution intended a befitting title in bestowing on the President of the United States the office of Commander in Chief of the land and naval forces, and nothing more. If they had intended to confer on him any supreme command to be exercised as a constitutional right, they would not have reserved to Congress the power to govern the Army, and require him "to see that the laws of Congress were faithfully executed."

If, in fact, the Constitution had conferred on the President the command of the Army and Navy, and added to his other executive functions of patronage, appointment, and the exchequer of the Government, the prerogative of the sword, his powers would have been more dangerous to liberty than any ever before exercised by any monarch since regal Rome was disintegrated by the military dominion of its Cesars.

But such was not the polity or intention of the framers of the Constitution, and no such powers have been conferred on the President, by implication or otherwise; but, on the contrary, all such authority is positively interdicted to him by section 14, Article I, Constitution, and vested in Congress.

What the General's powers are, should therefore, in my judgment, be more clearly enumerated in this article. As it now reads, paragraph 1, standing alone, would fix properly the military status of the General in Chief of the Army. But, by the qualifications in paragraphs 2, 3, and 4, that will permit the Secretary of War at any time, as the representative of the President, to interfere with the military orders of the General in Chief, only requiring orders of the Secretary of War, through the General as a military channel, to be published that may "otherwise direct," all the military operations of the Army may be obstructed, and every order the General may issue to-day can be canceled to-morrow by the paramount order of the Secretary of War.

In military laws, regulations, and orders, there should be neither vagueness, ambiguity, or possible misinterpretation, so that conflict of authority or antagonism in command can be made reasonably possible. Every commander's status should be clearly defined, in order that harmony in the execution of military administration shall be unalterably fixed. In this way alone can the efficiency of armies be established, and uniform discipline and justice enforced.

I would therefore suggest that paragraphs 2, 3, and 4, in Article III, be stricken out and the following substituted: "In all matters relating to the fiscal administration of the Army, the Secretary of War has supreme control, and he alone is responsible for the faithful and prompt settlement of all disbursing officers' accounts, and the economical application of the public moneys appropriated for the Army. So far as payments and disbursements are made at military posts to troops, or on account of military supplies, or for military movements, it is made the duty of the General commanding to see that they are made in conformity with the regulations and orders of the Secretary of War."

The office of the Secretary of War has grown into great proportions of power through enormous patronage by the contract system for vast supplies of war; and if to this power is superadded military dictation, it would, in the hands of an unfaithful, unscrupulous, or ambitious Secretary, become one of danger to liberty, and its doors would be thrown ajar to fraud and corruption, with military force to give it impunity and freedom from search.

The office of the senior General of the Army, by its very nature and life-tenure, is more identified with the paramount interests of the Army than any other, and very greatly transcends in its military reach into the discipline and effectiveness of the personnel of the rank and file, than that of the Secretary of War. Besides, it is unassociated with political and partisan interests, with patronage and its mischievous influences, than that of the Secretary of War; the latter being an office changing at brief periods, and never identified exclusively with purely military matters and their progression and improvements in the art and science of war. The General is an educated soldier, has exclusively the interests of his profession at heart, knows more intimately the personnel of the Army than the Secretary of War possibly can, and his pride and ambition are to elevate arms, and give to his Army its maximum of efficiency and discipline.

Political and personal favoritism are the banes of armies, and, if exercised in any considerable degree, are more destructive of military merit, *esprit* of profession, than all other disturbing elements in military administration. They are much more likely to find their way into service through a Secretary of War than through an old Army General, whose office is not transient, or in any way influenced by the inducements of popular applause or political favor.

Fifth. In fourth line, paragraph 2, Article IV, strike out the words "Secretary of War" and substitute the word "President." If this paragraph stands uncorrected it would confer military function on the Secretary of War in person. He is a civil officer, and can not, without the direction of the President, and as his aid, give any military orders. This part, as it now stands, submits grave military subjects to the "discretion of the Secretary of War," regardless of the President.

Sixth. Insert in Article I an additional paragraph, in these words: "Wherever in these regulations the words 'Secretary of War' are used, they will be construed as meaning the representative minister of the President in his executive office as Commander in Chief of the Army." This will give authorization to all of his orders as emanating directly from the President as the military head of the land forces.

Seventh. In paragraph 4, Article IX, strike out the words "the engineers" at the end of the third line, and in paragraph 5 strike out the words "whether superior or," in fourth line. Engineers should not command troops where there is a regimental commissioned officer, nor should a superior officer salute his junior officer because he is an adjutant. Besides, if the engineer officer can assume command by virtue of paragraph 4, then paragraph 10, same article, is stultified and inoperative.

Eighth. In paragraph 6, Article XIV, strike out the words "Secretary of War," in fourth line, and substitute for them "General of the Army." And also strike out the words "War Department" in paragraph 15, fourth line, and substitute for them "General of the Army." In Article XV strike out the words "War Department" from paragraph 1, second line, and substitute "General of the Army," and strike out "Secretary of War" from fifth line of paragraph 3 and substitute "General of the Army."

Ninth. On page 33, article headed "Grooming," strike out all of first paragraph and substitute the following: "Every commissioned officer of a troop of cavalry or mounted battery of artillery, not sick or prevented by other duty, will attend morning and evening stable-call, and personally superintend the thorough grooming, the feeding and watering of the horses. When the grooming is finished the horses should be formed in line by the noncommissioned officers in charge of squads, with the men at position 'stand to horse;' when the officers, accompanied by the blacksmith, shall inspect each horse and require regrooming if it has not been thoroughly done, and bring to the notice of the blacksmith horses that have cast their shoes or require reshoeing. They should also at this inspection see that every soldier is present with his horse, unless detained by sickness or on other indispensable duty he can not leave." As a rule, every soldier of a troop of cavalry or mounted battery of artillery, not on guard or in hospital, should be required to attend stable-call and groom, water, and feed his own horse. Affection and confidence between soldier and horse would in this manner be cultivated, so that the saying "the horse knoweth his rider" might be realized. The old cavalry rule, "horse and rider should never be separated," is the only safe law for making good cavalry.

Tenth. First paragraph of Article XXXIII makes "commanders of regiments responsible for the instruction and discipline of their regiments." Paragraph 8, however, completely stultifies paragraph 1, or at least makes it inoperative by its restrictions on their rights to inspect companies serving with other commanders. They can not inspect companies of their regiments serving at other posts oftener than once a year, and then only by virtue of orders from the General of the Army. This is all well enough as applied to artillery and infantry regimental commanders, in whose regiments the details of duties and administration of different posts should be under regulations identically the same. But when cavalry companies are serving at infantry or artillery posts, as the regimental duties of cavalry differ materially from the regimental duties of artillery and infantry, the regimental regulations and orders of cavalry commanders should be enforced, whoever may be in command of the post.

I would, therefore, suggest to except out of the operation of this paragraph 8 all cavalry troops and commands, and make a proviso, that whenever cavalry companies are serving at posts commanded by infantry or artillery officers, that so far as the cavalry regulations for interior cavalry administration and duties are concerned, that the regimental commanders of cavalry be fully authorized to enforce regimental orders and discipline.

Eleventh. It is certain that regimental commanders of cavalry should not be held responsible for the discipline or efficiency of their regiments, if their companies, serving at posts commanded by artillery or infantry officers, are placed beyond the enforcement of cavalry rules for such discipline and efficiency. The nature, organization, and distinctive characterization of these different arms of service are broad in differences, and the rules of a post for the enforcement of discipline and effectiveness in infantry and artillery would be wholly inadequate as applied to cavalry.

Twelfth. There is no reason for the discrimination between cavalry and mounted artillery, as made in mixed commands on page 112, paragraphs 6, 7, and 10, and to correct it, strike out paragraph 6, and in paragraph 7, after the words "mounted artillery," in first line, add, "and cavalry," and after the words "soldiers of mounted batteries," in first line of paragraph 10, add, "and cavalry." The service of a cavalry soldier, including the care of his additional equipments, arms, and hard scouting and escort duty, exceeds in its labor and fatigue that of a soldier of mounted artillery, in the care of horses and battery.

ARTICLES OF WAR.

Thirteenth. Article VI of the Rules and Articles of War, in its connection with Article XII, requires an additional paragraph in Article LXIV, which should read: "Whenever a general court-martial assembles, and before the prisoner is called upon by the judge-advocate to plead as to his guilt or innocence of the charges, if the judge-advocate finds in the array of the members a sufficient number of officers senior in rank to the prisoner to constitute a lawful court of five or more members, it shall be his duty to excuse the other members of the array from sitting, and thus avoid the influence of juniors, in trials where no other motive than to do justice should bear in forming the judgment of the court."

Article VI makes any number of officers from five to thirteen a lawful court for the trial of a commissioned officer, only requiring the maximum number thirteen, when that number can be convened without manifest injury to the service.

Article XII says "no officer shall be tried but by a general court-martial, nor by officers of an inferior rank, if it can be avoided without detriment to the public service." The policy of this law of courts is to move out of the juror's mind every motive that could operate to the prejudice of the prisoner to be tried, and as promotion of a junior follows by dismission of a senior officer, and the benefit of such promotion could possibly actuate the vote of a junior, the law in positive terms forbids the trial of a senior by a junior, "if it can be avoided without manifest injury to the service."

When five or more seniors constitute in part the panel of a court-martial, it is clear that a trial can be had by seniors, and Article XII applying in that case, the duty of the judge-advocate is to excuse the juniors, as otherwise the trial would be unlawful.

The object of Article XII is to secure purity in the administration of military justice in the Army, and that object would be accomplished with a greater degree of certainty by the additional paragraph I propose to add in defining the duties of the judge-advocate. He is the law officer of the Government in its military administration of justice, and all military jurists and writers agree that it is his duty, before proceeding to the trial of any officer, "to see that the court is legally constituted." As a rule, however, the judge-advocates of military courts are officers without erudition in law, or any great experience even in the administration of military justice. It is therefore of primary importance to fix the legal constitution of the courts so plainly, that the most inexperienced judge-advocates can not mistake the cardinal principle of its lawful organization, before putting military reputation or military officers "in jeopardy of life or limb."

Military honor is of peculiar characterization, and if once damaged, whether by mistake or otherwise, it is seldom so retrieved as to restore to full usefulness the officer on whose character a shadow has been cast.

The judgment of military courts should, therefore, be freed from all suspicion of inducement or motive to prevent justice, to disguise wrong, to impute innocence, or to convict of crime.

Fourteenth. In Article XVI, I would suggest substituting the word "shall" for "may," in line 6, that reads "and a court of inquiry may be ordered by any general," etc., so that it will read "shall be ordered," etc., because in my judgment it is the absolute right of an officer, when he thinks an imputation rests upon him, to acquit himself of it by such a court. When an officer's reputation is at all in question, his usefulness is at an end unless he can show that the imputation is groundless, and place himself above suspicion. It may often happen that the imputation comes directly or indirectly from the general or commanding officer on whom the demand is made for the court of inquiry by the injured officer. It should not therefore be left at the discretion of such general or commanding officer to refuse the application of the officers they may have wronged, as it would now seem to be by using the language "may be ordered." etc., as such language may be construed to leave the ordering of the court discretionary in their judgment. Military reputation can not rest under equivocation or in doubt; it must be unclouded, and courts of inquiry should never be refused, when demanded by any officer whose military character is under aspersion going to the integrity of his personal or official manhood.

APPENDIX II.

LETTER OF LIEUTENANT GENERAL SCHOFIELD IN REGARD TO PROPOSED REGULATIONS OF 1876.

ST. AUGUSTINE, FLA., *January 10, 1896.*

* * * In reply to your inquiry of January 8th, my recollection is that Col. Robt. Scott and Colonel Tourtellotte went on and completed the revision of regulations as I had mapped them out in the "first articles." I know that great progress had been made in that work when I ceased to supervise it, or give any further directions. In fact, the work after that was little more than clerical, the theory of it being that the drafts of staff regulations and the old general regulations should not be altered except so far as necessary to make them conform to the principles laid down in the first articles. I recollect that General Sherman wanted me to go on and complete the staff regulations without consulting the chiefs of staff departments, but I was not willing to do that, and all the chiefs, as I recollect, sent me their projects in detail. Of course these required much attention, and Colonel Scott was engaged in that work when my direction of it ceased. To this there was one, and as I recollect only one, exception. General Meigs, Quartermaster General, cordially adopted the theory laid down in one of the first articles attempting to define the relations between the Secretary of War, the General of the Army, and the chiefs of staff, which, he said, in substance, was the best definition he had ever seen of that relation.

It may be of interest in your history to note that the relation there attempted to be defined was not any invention of mine, but was what I understood to have been General Grant's idea when he was in command of the Army, and that of General Sherman when he ordered me to revise the regulations. I was simply called upon to act as a sort of expert, to put in form those views of my superiors. I was not at liberty to embody in that revision any independent views of my own, even if I had any at that time. But my recollection is that I did not have at that time, any thought on the subject but to carry out as well I could the will of my superiors, the General in Chief and the President, who I presumed were in perfect accord, their previous differences having then resulted in the resignation of Secretary Belknap, and the restoration of General Sherman to *actual* command.

My own independent and matured views are to be found in communications addressed to the President when I was in command of the Army, now, doubtless, on the files of the War Department, either public or confidential.

I presume all the work done by Colonel Scott and Colonel Tourtellotte on that revision is somewhere in the War Department or Army Headquarters.

* * * * * *

Yours, very truly,

J. M. SCHOFIELD.

APPENDIX I.

REMARKS OF SECRETARY OF WAR McCRARY, IN HIS ANNUAL REPORT FOR 1877.

ARMY REGULATIONS.

The latest revision of the regulations for the government of the Army was made in 1861, to which some additions were made in 1863. The regulations then adopted were published in 1863, but are now out of print, and besides have been supplemented by numerous general and special orders and modified by various legislative acts, so that it may be said that there is great need of a careful revision of the whole subject. The attempts heretofore made to supply the need which is generally felt in the Army of a new and complete code of regulations have not resulted in success, although much work has been done which may be utilized hereafter.

By an act approved July 28, 1866, the Secretary of War was directed to have prepared and to report to Congress at the next session "a code of regulations for the government of the Army and of the militia in actual service, which shall embrace all necessary orders and forms of a general character for the performance of all duties incumbent on officers and men in the military service, including rules for the government of courts martial; the existing regulations to remain in force until Congress shall have acted on said report." In compliance with the terms of this act, a revision of the Rules and Articles of War was made and submitted to Congress, but no action was taken thereon.

By an act approved July 15, 1870, it was again provided that a system of general regulations for the Army therein authorized should be reported to Congress at the next session and approved by that body.

The act of March 1, 1875, vol. 18, Statutes at Large, page 337, repealed so much of said act of July 15, 1870, as required regulations to be submitted to Congress, and authorized the President "to make and publish regulations for the government of the Army in accordance with existing laws."

By an act approved July 24, 1876 (19 Stat., p. 101), the whole subject-matter of reform and reorganization of the Army of the United States was referred to a commission, to be composed of two members of the Senate, two members of the House of Representatives, two officers of the Army from the line, one officer of the Army from the staff, and the Secretary of War. This commission was to report to Congress at its next session. By a joint resolution approved August 15, 1876 (19 Stat., p. 216), the President was requested to postpone all action in connection with the publication of regulations until after the report of the commission above mentioned should be received and acted on by Congress at its next session. The commission, however, adjourned, after collecting a great mass of material, without accomplishing its object, not being able to complete its work before the Congress to which it was required to report had expired.

Thus it will be seen that the powers of the commission have been exhausted, while at the same time the law is left in such a state as to render it extremely doubtful as to the power of the Executive to issue and publish regulations. It will be for Congress to determine whether it is wise to require that a code of general regulations shall be subjected to the formal action of Congress, thus giving them a fixed character, unalterable except by the same formal action. In my judgment, this would not be wise. All matter in the regulations which should properly be bound by force of law is actually made in exact conformity with military acts of Congress, and is always in the precise language of the statutes; but there are very many matters of detail which depend upon the daily changing necessities of the service, and are regulated by the experience and intelligence of practical men in the Army, which should be left for modification, as often as circumstances demand, to the discretion of the Executive. It is a principle, well understood and invariably acted upon, that whenever a regulation comes in conflict with a law of Congress, it is null and void. The law is thus, as it were, a constitution, and regulations are simply the by-laws based thereon.

The authority to make alterations in the regulations was vested by act of April 24, 1816, in the Secretary of War, with the approval of the President, and has been ever since so exercised, with this exception, that by an act of March 2, 1821, a system prepared by General Scott, under an act of March 3, 1813, was "approved and adopted." But this act of March 2, 1821, was repealed, in terms, by an act of May 7, 1822, leaving the act of April 24, 1816, still in operation. The Army regulations are always public and easy of reference, and Congress can readily, at any time, correct by legislation any objectionable feature which may appear in them.

o

www.ingramcontent.com/pod-product-compliance
Lightning Source LLC
Chambersburg PA
CBHW032142160426
43197CB00008B/742